W9-DBA-727

WeightWatchers®

In No Time

A Word About Weight Watchers

Since 1963, Weight Watchers has grown from a handful of people to millions of enrollments annually. Today, Weight Watchers is recognized as the leading name in safe and sensible weight control. Weight Watchers members form diverse groups, from youths to senior citizens, attending meetings virtually around the globe. Weight-loss and weight-management results vary by individual, but we recommend that you attend Weight Watchers meetings to benefit from the supportive environment you'll find there and follow the comprehensive Weight Watchers program which includes food plans, an activity plan, and a thinking skills plan. For the Weight Watchers meeting nearest you, call **800-651-6000**. For information on bringing Weight Watchers to your workplace, call **800-8AT-WORK.** Also, visit us at our Web site, **WeightWatchers.com**, or look for *Weight Watchers* Magazine at your newsstand or in your meeting room.

 **Core Plan** recipe

Tuscan Chicken Sausage
Stew, page 97

WEIGHT WATCHERS PUBLISHING GROUP

CREATIVE AND EDITORIAL DIRECTOR	**NANCY GAGLIARDI**
ART DIRECTOR	**ED MELNITSKY**
PRODUCTION MANAGER	**ALAN BIEDERMAN**
ASSOCIATE ART DIRECTOR	**JENNIFER BOWLES**
OFFICE MANAGER AND PUBLISHING ASSISTANT	**JENNY LABOY-BRACE**
FOOD EDITOR	**EILEEN RUNYAN**
FOOD CONSULTANT	**CAROL PRAGER**
RECIPE DEVELOPERS	**DAVID BONOM**
	TERRY GREICO-KENNY
	WENDY KALEN
	MARK SCARBROUGH
	BRUCE WEINSTEIN
NUTRITION CONSULTANT	**U. BEATE KRINKE**
PHOTOGRAPHER	**RITA MAAS**
FOOD STYLIST	**MICHAEL PEDERSON**
PROP STYLIST	**CATHY COOK**
DESIGN/PRODUCTION	**LYNDA D'AMICO**

ON THE COVER: Pasta with Sausage, Spinach, and Pine Nuts, page 112 (with a *POINTS*® value of only 7)

Copyright © 2006 Weight Watchers International, Inc. Nothing may be reprinted
in whole or in part without permission from the publisher. Editorial and art produced by
W/W Twentyfirst Corp., 747 Third Ave., NY, NY 10017.
WEIGHT WATCHERS is a registered trademark of Weight Watchers International, Inc.
SKU #0011126 Printed in the USA

About Our Recipes

We make every effort to ensure that you will have success with our recipes. For best results and for nutritional accuracy, please keep the following guidelines in mind:

● Recipes in this book have been developed for Weight Watchers members who are following either the **Core Plan** or the **Flex Plan** on the TurnAround® program. All **Core Plan** recipes are marked with our **Core Plan** recipe icon ☑. We include *POINTS*® values so you can use any of the recipes if you are following the **Flex Plan** on the program. *POINTS* values are assigned based on calories, fat (grams), and fiber (grams) provided for a serving size of a recipe.

● All recipes feature approximate nutritional information; our recipes are analyzed for Calories (Cal), Total Fat (Fat), Saturated Fat (Sat Fat), Trans Fat (Trans Fat), Cholesterol (Chol), Sodium (Sod), Carbohydrates (Carb), Dietary Fiber (Fib), Protein (Prot), and Calcium (Calc).

● Nutritional information for recipes that include meat, poultry, and fish are based on cooked skinless boneless portions (unless otherwise stated), with the fat trimmed.

● We recommend that you buy lean meat and poultry, then trim it of all visible fat before cooking. When poultry is cooked with the skin on, we suggest removing the skin before eating.

● Before serving, divide foods—including any vegetables, sauce, or accompaniments—into portions of equal size according to the designated number of servings per recipe.

● Any substitutions made to the ingredients will alter the "Per serving" nutritional information and may affect the **Core Plan** recipe status or the *POINTS* value.

● It is implied that all fresh fruits, vegetables, and greens in recipes should be rinsed before using.

Asian Salmon Strips with Watercress
and Scallions, page 119

Contents

Appetizers and Lite Bites

p 12, 14, 15

p 21

CHAPTER 1

Smoked Salmon and Horseradish Dip

HANDS-ON PREP **15 MIN**
COOK **NONE**
SERVES **6**

Put half the salmon, the sour cream, dill, horseradish, lemon juice, and pepper in a food processor or blender; pulse just to combine. Transfer to a small bowl, then stir in the remaining salmon.

PER SERVING (¼ cup): 74 Cal, 5 g Fat, 3 g Sat Fat, 0 g Trans Fat, 19 mg Chol, 168 mg Sod, 2 g Carb, 0 g Fib, 4 g Prot, 43 mg Calc. **POINTS** value: *2.*

HOW WE DID IT Be sure not to over process the ingredients in the food processor—you want to have small bits of the salmon throughout the dip for added body and texture.

¼ **pound** smoked salmon, chopped

1 **(8-ounce) container** light sour cream

1 **tablespoon chopped** fresh dill

1½ **teaspoons** prepared horseradish

1 **teaspoon** fresh lemon juice

⅛ **teaspoon** freshly ground pepper

Shrimp and Jicama Salsa

HANDS-ON PREP **15 MIN**
COOK **NONE**
SERVES **12**

Combine the shrimp, jicama, lime juice, onion, mint, oil, salt, and hot pepper sauce in a medium bowl. Serve at once or cover and refrigerate for up to 8 hours.

PER SERVING (¼ cup): 33 Cal, 1 g Fat, 0 g Sat Fat, 0 g Trans Fat, 37 mg Chol, 68 mg Sod, 3 g Carb, 1 g Fib, 4 g Prot, 11 mg Calc. **POINTS** value: **1**.

GOOD IDEA Belgian endive spears are great for scooping up this salsa. Tortilla chips are excellent, as well; count on 6 baked low-fat chips for each guest (you'll increase the per-serving **POINTS** value by 1 and you'll need to deduct them from your weekly **POINTS** Allowance).

½ **pound** cooked peeled and deveined shrimp, coarsely chopped

½ **medium jicama,** peeled and diced

2 **tablespoons** fresh lime juice

1 **tablespoon minced** red onion

1 **tablespoon chopped** fresh mint

1 **teaspoon** olive oil

⅛ **teaspoon** salt

⅛ **teaspoon** hot pepper sauce

Beef Crostini with Arugula

HANDS-ON PREP **10 MIN**
COOK **2 MIN**
SERVES **8**

1 Preheat the broiler. Arrange the baguette slices on the broiler rack and broil 3 inches from the heat until lightly browned, about 45 seconds on each side.

2 Spread each baguette slice with ¼ teaspoon of the tapenade; top each with ½ arugula leaf and 1 piece roast beef. Serve at once.

PER SERVING (3 crostini): 104 Cal, 2 g Fat, 1 g Sat Fat, 0 g Trans Fat, 12 mg Chol, 304 mg Sod, 14 g Carb, 1 g Fib, 7 g Prot, 28 mg Calc. **_POINTS_** value: **_2._**

TRY IT Tapenade (TA-puh-nahd) is a thick paste made in France from capers, anchovies, ripe olives, olive oil, and lemon juice. It packs a lot of flavor, so you only need to use a tiny bit as a spread. Look for tapenade in gourmet food shops or with the condiments in larger supermarkets.

½ **baguette, cut diagonally into 24 (¼-inch-thick) slices**

2 **tablespoons jarred tapenade (black olive paste)**

12 **medium arugula leaves, each torn in half**

6 **thin slices (¼ pound) deli roast beef, cut crosswise into quarters**

Almond Shrimp in Endive
Leaves (page 14), Roasted Red
Pepper Bruschetta (page 15),
and Beef Crostini with Arugula

Almond Shrimp in Endive Leaves

HANDS-ON PREP **10 MIN**
COOK **3 MIN**
SERVES **10**

1 Heat a medium nonstick skillet over medium heat. Add the almonds and cook, stirring frequently, until golden and fragrant, about 3 minutes. Let cool slightly.

2 Meanwhile, combine the shrimp, celery leaves, scallion, basil, vinegar, oil, salt, and pepper in a medium bowl. Stir the almonds into the shrimp mixture.

3 Arrange the endive leaves on a large serving platter; spoon about 1 tablespoon shrimp mixture onto each leaf.

PER SERVING (2 leaves): 42 Cal, 2 g Fat, 0 g Sat Fat, 0 g Trans Fat, 44 mg Chol, 113 mg Sod, 1 g Carb, 1 g Fib, 5 g Prot, 22 mg Calc. *POINTS* value: *1.*

¼ **cup** sliced almonds

½ **pound** cooked peeled and deveined shrimp, coarsely chopped

1 **tablespoon finely chopped** celery leaves

1 **tablespoon finely chopped** scallion

1 **tablespoon chopped** fresh basil

1 **tablespoon** white balsamic or white-wine vinegar

1 **teaspoon** extra-virgin olive oil

¼ **teaspoon** salt

⅛ **teaspoon** freshly ground pepper

2 Belgian endives, leaves separated

Roasted Red Pepper Bruschetta

HANDS-ON PREP **15 MIN**
COOK **4 MIN**
SERVES **10**

1 Preheat the broiler. Slice the baguette in half lengthwise and place cut-side up on the broiler rack.

2 Combine the bell peppers, olives, shallots, oil, vinegar, thyme, and pepper in a medium bowl. Spoon the mixture evenly over the cut sides of the baguette halves, then top evenly with the goat cheese. Broil 5 inches from the heat until the cheese begins to soften and the edges of the baguette are lightly browned, about 4 minutes. Cut each baguette half into 15 slices and serve warm.

PER SERVING (3 slices): 119 Cal, 4 g Fat, 1 g Sat Fat, 0 g Trans Fat, 3 mg Chol, 294 mg Sod, 17 g Carb, 1 g Fib, 4 g Prot, 40 mg Calc.
POINTS value: **3.**

GOOD IDEA To make this appetizer even more colorful, look for red and yellow roasted peppers.

- 1 (15-inch) sourdough baguette
- 2 (7-ounce) jars roasted red bell peppers, drained and sliced
- 12 pitted kalamata olives, coarsely chopped
- 2 tablespoons minced shallots
- 1 tablespoon extra-virgin olive oil
- 1 tablespoon balsamic vinegar
- ½ teaspoon dried thyme
- ¼ teaspoon freshly ground pepper
- 2 ounces goat cheese, crumbled

Crab and Cucumber Canapés

HANDS-ON PREP **20 MIN**
COOK **NONE**
SERVES **10**

Combine the mayonnaise, scallion, cilantro, lime juice, salt, and cayenne in a medium bowl. Stir in the crabmeat. Spoon 1 teaspoon of the crabmeat mixture onto each cucumber slice. Serve at once or cover and refrigerate for up to 3 hours.

PER SERVING (2 canapés): 17 Cal, 0 g Fat, 0 g Sat Fat, 0 g Trans Fat, 12 mg Chol, 77 mg Sod, 1 g Carb, 0 g Fib, 2 g Prot, 17 mg Calc. *POINTS* value: *0.*

FOOD NOTE There are two varieties of cooked crabmeat available—lump meat (whole pieces of the white body meat) or less expensive flaked meat (small bits of light and dark meat from the body and claws). Either is delicious in this recipe.

1 tablespoon + 1 teaspoon fat-free mayonnaise

1 tablespoon finely chopped scallion

1 tablespoon finely chopped fresh cilantro

2 teaspoons fresh lime juice

⅛ teaspoon salt

Pinch cayenne

¼ pound cooked fresh or frozen crabmeat, picked over for pieces of shell

1 seedless cucumber, cut into 20 (½-inch-thick) slices

Clams with Sherry Sauce

HANDS-ON PREP **5 MIN**
COOK **15 MIN**
SERVES **6**

Heat the oil in a medium Dutch oven over medium-high heat. Add the onion and ham; cook, stirring frequently, until lightly browned, about 5 minutes. Add the sherry and clams; bring to a boil. Reduce the heat to medium, cover, and steam until the clams open, about 8 minutes, stirring after 4 minutes. Discard any clams that do not open. Sprinkle the clams and sauce with the parsley. Serve at once.

PER SERVING (4 clams with 2 tablespoons sauce): 79 Cal, 2 g Fat, 0 g Sat Fat, 0 g Trans Fat, 24 mg Chol, 105 mg Sod, 4 g Carb, 0 g Fib, 9 g Prot, 31 mg Calc. *POINTS* value: *2.*

PLAY IT SAFE When buying clams, make sure the shells are tightly closed. If a shell is slightly open, tap it lightly. If it doesn't snap shut, the clam is dead and should be discarded. Also, the shells should be whole, not broken or cracked.

- 2 teaspoons olive oil
- ½ cup finely chopped onion
- ⅓ cup finely chopped reduced-sodium ham
- ¼ cup dry sherry
- 2 dozen littleneck clams, scrubbed
- 1 tablespoon chopped flat-leaf parsley

Speedy Avocado Salsa

HANDS-ON PREP **15 MIN**
COOK **NONE**
SERVES **6**

Combine the avocado, cucumber, salsa, and cilantro in a medium bowl. Serve at once or cover and refrigerate for up to 8 hours.

PER SERVING (⅓ cup): 54 Cal, 4 g Fat, 1 g Sat Fat, 0 g Trans Fat, 0 mg Chol, 65 mg Sod, 4 g Carb, 2 g Fib, 1 g Prot, 11 mg Calc. **POINTS** value: *1.*

FOOD NOTE The best way to tell if an avocado is ready to eat is to gently squeeze it in the palm of your hand. Ripe fruit will be firm yet will yield to gentle pressure.

1 **medium ripe avocado, halved, pitted, peeled, and diced**

¼ **seedless cucumber, diced**

⅓ **cup** bottled fat-free **salsa**

1 **tablespoon chopped** fresh cilantro

Sesame-Ginger Edamame

HANDS-ON PREP **10 MIN**
COOK **5 MIN**
SERVES **6**

Heat the oil in a large nonstick skillet over medium-high heat. Add the garlic, ginger, and crushed red pepper; cook, stirring frequently, until fragrant, about 30 seconds. Add the edamame and salt; cook, stirring, until heated through, about 4 minutes.

PER SERVING (about ½ cup): 76 Cal, 4 g Fat, 0 g Sat Fat, 0 g Trans Fat, 0 mg Chol, 54 mg Sod, 6 g Carb, 2 g Fib, 6 g Prot, 70 mg Calc. **POINTS** value: **1.**

TRY IT *Edamame* (eh-dah-MAH-meh), the Japanese name for soybeans, are harvested when the soybeans are still green and sweet tasting. *Edamame* is high in protein and fiber. It's available shelled and frozen in many supermarkets, and Asian or natural food stores.

1 teaspoon **Asian (dark) sesame oil**

1½ teaspoons **minced garlic**

1 teaspoon grated peeled **fresh ginger**

⅛ teaspoon **crushed red pepper**

1 (10-ounce) package frozen shelled **edamame (green soybeans), thawed**

⅛ teaspoon **salt**

Microwave Potato Nachos

Microwave Potato Nachos

HANDS-ON PREP **10 MIN**
COOK **8 MIN**
SERVES **4**

1 Cut the potato into ³⁄₈-inch-thick slices; arrange in a single layer in a microwavable dish. Sprinkle the potatoes with the cumin, salt, and pepper. Cover with plastic wrap, then prick a few holes in the plastic to vent. Microwave on High until tender, 6 minutes.

2 Spoon the salsa over the potatoes; sprinkle with the beans and cheese. Microwave, uncovered, on Medium until the cheese is melted, 1½–2 minutes. Sprinkle with the scallion and serve at once.

PER SERVING (3 nachos): 95 Cal, 1 g Fat, 0 g Sat Fat, 0 g Trans Fat, 2 mg Chol, 416 mg Sod, 17 g Carb, 3 g Fib, 5 g Prot, 104 mg Calc. *POINTS* value: *1.*

1 large baking potato, scrubbed

¼ teaspoon ground cumin

¼ teaspoon salt

¼ teaspoon freshly ground pepper

⅓ cup bottled chunky salsa

½ cup canned black beans, rinsed and drained

⅓ cup shredded reduced-fat cheddar cheese

1 scallion, sliced

Nut and Olive Quesadillas

HANDS-ON PREP **5 MIN**
COOK **15 MIN**
SERVES **8**

1 To make the filling, combine the mozzarella, feta, olives, walnuts, oregano, and pepper in a medium bowl.

2 Sprinkle the filling evenly on 3 of the tortillas (about ½ cup on each). Place the remaining 3 tortillas on top and press firmly. Lightly spray both sides of the quesadillas with nonstick spray.

3 Set a medium nonstick skillet over medium-high heat. Add 1 quesadilla and cook until crisp and heated through, about 2 minutes on each side. Repeat with the remaining quesadillas. Cut each quesadilla into eighths, making a total of 24 wedges.

PER SERVING (3 wedges): 128 Cal, 5 g Fat, 2 g Sat Fat, 0 g Trans Fat, 9 mg Chol, 405 mg Sod, 15 g Carb, 1 g Fib, 6 g Prot, 151 mg Calc. **POINTS** value: **3.**

EXPRESS LANE If you have a large griddle pan, save time and cook all three quesadillas together.

¾ **cup shredded** part-skim mozzarella cheese

½ **cup crumbled** reduced-fat feta cheese

2 **tablespoons finely chopped** pitted ripe black olives

2 **tablespoons finely chopped walnuts**

½ **teaspoon** dried oregano, **crushed**

¼ **teaspoon freshly ground pepper**

6 **(6-inch)** fat-free flour tortillas

Microwave Fruity Popcorn Mix

HANDS-ON PREP **5 MIN**

COOK **1 MIN**

SERVES **8**

1 Combine the oil, curry powder, ginger, and cayenne in a microwavable cup. Microwave on High until fragrant, 45–60 seconds.

2 Combine the popcorn, dried fruit morsels, and peanuts in a large bowl. Drizzle the spice mixture over the popcorn mixture and toss gently to coat.

PER SERVING (¾ cup): 94 Cal, 5 g Fat, 1 g Sat Fat, 0 g Trans Fat, 0 mg Chol, 51 mg Sod, 11 g Carb, 2 g Fib, 2 g Prot, 10 mg Calc. **POINTS** value: **2**.

GOOD IDEA Avoid using butter-flavored popcorn in this recipe, which is higher in fat and calories than plain popcorn. If you're popping the corn yourself, you'll need about ⅓ cup unpopped popcorn to yield 6 cups popped.

1 tablespoon olive oil

½ teaspoon curry powder

½ teaspoon ground ginger

Pinch cayenne

6 cups plain air-popped popcorn

½ cup mixed dried fruit morsels

⅓ cup dry-roasted peanuts

Light Brunches and Lunches

CHAPTER 2

Herb Shirred Eggs

HANDS-ON PREP **10 MIN**
COOK **10 MIN**
SERVES **4**

1 Preheat the oven to 375°F. Spray 4 (6-ounce) ovenproof, custard cups with nonstick spray.

2 Mix the thyme and parsley together in a small bowl. Sprinkle ¼ teaspoon of the herb mixture on the bottom of each custard cup. Gently, so as not to disturb the herbs, pour 2 teaspoons milk in each cup. Place the cups on a rimmed baking sheet.

3 Crack one egg into each cup, taking care to slip the egg in without breaking the yolk. Sprinkle ¼ teaspoon more herb mixture over each egg, then sprinkle ¼ teaspoon salt and some ground pepper over each. Bake until the whites are set and the yolks are warm but loose, about 10 minutes. If desired, bake 2–3 minutes longer to set the yolks.

PER SERVING (1 egg in a cup): 82 Cal, 5 g Fat, 2 g Sat Fat, 0 g Trans Fat, 212 mg Chol, 657 mg Sod, 1 g Carb, 0 g Fib, 7 g Prot, 40 mg Calc. *POINTS* value: *2.*

`GOOD IDEA` You might like to substitute other combinations of fresh, leafy herbs in similar quantities; try rosemary and oregano, or tarragon and chives. Or substitute ground dry herbs, such as ground cumin and chili powder, or curry powder and ground ginger. This recipe can also be doubled or tripled for large gatherings.

1 teaspoon minced
fresh thyme

1 teaspoon chopped
flat-leaf parsley

8 teaspoons **fat-free milk**

4 large **eggs**

1 teaspoon **salt**

Freshly ground pepper

Eggs, Lox, and Onions

HANDS-ON PREP **5 MIN**
COOK **10 MIN**
SERVES **4**

1 Melt the butter in a large nonstick skillet over low heat. Add the onions and cook, stirring, until golden, about 7 minutes. Meanwhile, whisk the eggs, egg whites, and milk in a small bowl until frothy.

2 Raise the heat to medium-high. Pour the egg mixture over the softened onions, swirl to cover the pan, and cook, undisturbed, about 15 seconds. Add the lox and cook, stirring frequently, until set, about 30 seconds. Season the eggs with the pepper. Divide evenly among 4 plates. Top each serving with 1 tablespoon sour cream and 1 teaspoon chopped chives.

PER SERVING (about ⅔ cup scrambled egg mixture and 1 tablespoon sour cream): 138 Cal, 5 g Fat, 2 g Sat Fat, 0 g Trans Fat, 117 mg Chol, 351 mg Sod, 8 g Carb, 1 g Fib, 14 g Prot, 64 mg Calc.
POINTS** value: **3.

HOW WE DID IT The trick to great scrambled eggs is not to overcook them: The second the eggs are no longer runny, remove them from the heat. To find the best smoked salmon, go to a fish market where the fishmonger will slice it to order off the side of salmon. Ask for thin slices from the middle, if possible. Failing this, look for vacuum-sealed pouches of salmon at the fish counter of most supermarkets.

1 **teaspoon** unsalted butter

2 **medium onions,** chopped

2 **large eggs**

5 **egg whites**

3 **tablespoons fat-free milk**

¼ **pound** lox or smoked salmon, **chopped**

Freshly ground pepper

4 **tablespoons** fat-free sour cream

4 **teaspoons chopped chives** or chopped scallions, **green part only**

Spicy Beans and Greens Omelette

HANDS-ON PREP **5 MIN**
COOK **5 MIN**
SERVES **2**

1 Heat the taco sauce, pinto beans, and spinach in a medium nonstick saucepan, stirring occasionally, until the spinach wilts, about 2 minutes.

2 Meanwhile, spray a 10-inch nonstick skillet with nonstick spray and set over medium-high heat. Pour in the egg substitute and swirl to cover the pan. Cook, stirring gently, until the underside is set, about 20 seconds. Lifting the edges frequently with a spatula to let the uncooked egg flow underneath, cook 30 seconds more.

3 Spread the spinach mixture evenly over half the omelette; fold the other half over the filling. Slide the omelette onto a plate.

PER SERVING (½ omelette): 78 Cal, 0 g Fat, 0 g Sat Fat, 0 g Trans Fat, 0 mg Chol, 323 mg Sod, 10 g Carb, 4 g Fib, 10 g Prot, 82 mg Calc. ***POINTS*** value: **1.**

¼ cup **bottled taco sauce**

¼ cup **canned pinto beans, rinsed and drained**

3 cups **lightly packed baby spinach leaves (about 3 ounces)**

½ cup **fat-free egg substitute**

Aegean Frittata

HANDS-ON PREP **5 MIN**
COOK **15 MIN**
SERVES **4**

1 Heat the oil in a large nonstick skillet over medium-high heat. Add the potatoes, onion, bell pepper, oregano, salt, and pepper. Cook, stirring frequently, until the vegetables are tender and golden, about 6 minutes.

2 Meanwhile, lightly beat the eggs and egg whites in a medium bowl. Reduce the heat under the skillet to medium; add the eggs and cook until almost set, lifting the edges frequently with a spatula to let the uncooked egg flow underneath, about 3 minutes.

3 Sprinkle the feta cheese over the frittata. Cover the skillet; reduce the heat to low and cook until the cheese melts slightly, about 3 minutes. Cut into 4 wedges.

PER SERVING (1 wedge): 175 Cal, 8 g Fat, 2 g Sat Fat, 0 g Trans Fat, 163 mg Chol, 443 mg Sod, 14 g Carb, 2 g Fib, 10 g Prot, 58 mg Calc. **POINTS** value: **4.**

GOOD IDEA You could substitute other vegetables in this frittata, such as zucchini, chopped broccoli, or tomatoes, and other cheeses, such as cheddar or Monterey Jack.

1 tablespoon olive oil

1 cup frozen hash-brown potatoes

½ cup chopped frozen onion

½ cup chopped frozen green bell pepper

1 teaspoon dried oregano

¼ teaspoon salt

¼ teaspoon ground black pepper

3 large eggs

4 egg whites

2 tablespoons crumbled feta cheese

Crab Frittata

1 Spray a 10-inch nonstick skillet with nonstick spray and set over medium-high heat. Add the scallions and bell pepper; cook, stirring, until softened, about 2 minutes.

2 Sprinkle the crab, salt, and pepper over the vegetables; cook, stirring, about 30 seconds. Pour in the egg substitute and swirl to cover the pan.

3 Cover and reduce the heat to low. Cook until set, about 9 minutes. Run a spatula under the frittata to loosen it from the pan. Slide onto a serving plate and cut into 6 wedges.

PER SERVING (⅙ of frittata): 71 Cal, 1 g Fat, 0 g Sat Fat, 0 g Trans Fat, 28 mg Chol, 394 mg Sod, 4 g Carb, 1 g Fib, 13 g Prot, 64 mg Calc. **POINTS** value: **1.**

FOOD NOTE Crabmeat can be found refrigerated at the fish counter of many supermarkets, usually in plastic containers. Be sure to check the expiration date for maximum freshness.

7 scallions, thinly sliced

1 red bell pepper, seeded and chopped

6 ounces cooked fresh lump crabmeat, picked over for pieces of shell

½ teaspoon salt

Freshly ground pepper

1½ cups fat-free egg substitute

Crab Frittata

Scrambled Tortilla Eggs with Taco Sauce

HANDS-ON PREP **5 MIN**
COOK **15 MIN**
SERVES **4**

1 Cut each tortilla in half, then crosswise into 6 strips, making a total of 48 strips.

2 Heat the oil in a large nonstick skillet over medium-high heat. Add the tortilla strips and cook, tossing frequently, until crisp and golden, about 5 minutes. Transfer the strips to a plate.

3 Add the onion to the same skillet and cook over medium heat, stirring occasionally, until golden, about 5 minutes. Add the egg substitute, cheese, and chiles; cook, stirring occasionally, until the eggs are slightly set, about 2 minutes. Stir in the tortilla strips and cook until the eggs are scrambled and firm, about 2 minutes longer. Serve at once with the taco sauce and cilantro.

PER SERVING (¾ cup scrambled egg mixture and 2 tablespoons taco sauce): 243 Cal, 9 g Fat, 4 g Sat Fat, 0 g Trans Fat, 19 mg Chol, 734 mg Sod, 19 g Carb, 4 g Fib, 22 g Prot, 304 mg Calc.
POINTS value: **5.**

- 4 (6-inch) corn tortillas
- 2 teaspoons canola oil
- ¾ cup chopped onion
- 2 cups fat-free egg substitute
- 1 cup shredded reduced-fat pepperjack cheese
- 1 (4-ounce) can chopped mild green chiles
- ½ cup bottled taco sauce
- 2 tablespoons coarsely chopped fresh cilantro

Egg Foo Yong

HANDS-ON PREP **10 MIN**
COOK **5 MIN**
SERVES **4**

1 Lightly beat the eggs, egg whites, soy sauce, salt, and pepper in a medium bowl; set aside.

2 Heat a large nonstick skillet or wok over medium-high heat until a drop of water sizzles. Pour in the oil and swirl to coat the pan. Add the scallions and celery; stir-fry 1 minute. Add the bean sprouts and bamboo shoots; stir-fry until the vegetables are crisp-tender, about 2 minutes. Add the egg mixture and stir-fry until the eggs are just set, 1–2 minutes. Serve sprinkled with the cilantro.

PER SERVING (scant 1 cup): 162 Cal, 9 g Fat, 2 g Sat Fat, 0 g Trans Fat, 159 mg Chol, 634 mg Sod, 7 g Carb, 2 g Fib, 16 g Prot, 65 mg Calc. **POINTS** value: **4.**

FOOD NOTE Bean sprouts often come in 12-ounce bags, so if you have extra, be aware that they will keep for only 2 to 3 days, stored in the refrigerator. Stir-fry bean sprouts in a large skillet with sesame oil and a good shake of salt for a quick side dish.

3 **large eggs**

6 **egg whites**

1 **teaspoon reduced-sodium soy sauce**

¾ **teaspoon salt**

¼ **teaspoon freshly ground pepper**

2 **teaspoons Asian (dark) sesame oil**

4 **scallions, sliced on the diagonal**

1 **celery stalk, thinly sliced on the diagonal**

2 **cups fresh bean sprouts**

1 **(8-ounce) can bamboo shoot strips, drained**

2 **tablespoons chopped fresh cilantro or parsley**

Breakfast Burrito

HANDS-ON PREP **5 MIN**
COOK **8 MIN**
SERVES **4**

1 Layer the tortillas between sheets of wax paper; microwave on High until warm, 25 seconds.

2 Spray a medium nonstick skillet with nonstick spray and set over medium-high heat. Add the black beans and chili powder; cook until heated through, about 5 minutes. Add the egg substitute and cook, stirring frequently, until set, about 3 minutes.

3 Fill each tortilla with ¼ of the egg mixture, then top each with 1 tablespoon cheese and 1 tablespoon salsa. Roll the burritos closed.

PER SERVING (1 burrito): 342 Cal, 3 g Fat, 1 g Sat Fat, 0 g Trans Fat, 5 mg Chol, 1203 mg Sod, 59 g Carb, 11 g Fib, 24 g Prot, 207 mg Calc. **POINTS** value: **6.**

GOOD IDEA Don't just think of this dish as a **weekday convenience. For an elegant breakfast, serve these burritos alongside a bowl of raspberries, blueberries, and sliced strawberries, drizzled with a little reduced-fat poppy seed dressing.**

4 (10-inch) fat-free whole-wheat tortillas

1 cup canned black beans, rinsed and drained

1½ teaspoons chili powder

1 cup fat-free egg substitute

4 tablespoons shredded reduced-fat Mexican cheese blend

4 tablespoons bottled salsa, preferably a fruit salsa

Buckwheat Pancakes

HANDS-ON PREP **5 MIN**
COOK **15 MIN**
SERVES **6**

1 Combine the egg, egg white, buttermilk, applesauce, oil, and honey in a large bowl. Combine the flour, buckwheat flour, baking powder, and salt in another bowl. Stir the flour mixture into the buttermilk mixture just until blended.

2 Spray a large nonstick griddle or skillet with nonstick spray and set over medium-low heat. Pour the batter by ¼-cup measures into the skillet. Cook until bubbles just begin to appear at the edges of the pancakes, about 2 minutes. Flip and cook about 1 minute longer. Repeat with the remaining batter, making a total of 12 pancakes.

PER SERVING (2 pancakes): 173 Cal, 5 g Fat, 1 g Sat Fat, 0 g Trans Fat, 37 mg Chol, 423 mg Sod, 27 g Carb, 2 g Fib, 6 g Prot, 149 mg Calc. *POINTS* value: *3*.

EXPRESS LANE Not enough time on a busy morning? Combine the egg mixture and the flour mixture the night before in separate bowls. Store the egg mixture, covered, in the refrigerator overnight and let the flour mixture stand on the counter.

- **1 large** egg
- **1 egg white**
- **1 cup low-fat buttermilk**
- **½ cup unsweetened applesauce**
- **1½ tablespoons canola oil**
- **1 tablespoon honey**
- **¾ cup all-purpose flour**
- **½ cup buckwheat flour**
- **2 teaspoons baking powder**
- **½ teaspoon salt**

Berry Breakfast Crêpes

Berry Breakfast Crêpes

HANDS-ON PREP **10 MIN**
COOK **10 MIN**
SERVES **4**

1 Toss the raspberries, blueberries, 2 teaspoons of the sugar, and the lemon juice in a medium bowl; set aside.

2 To make the crêpes, beat the egg, evaporated milk, melted butter, vanilla, salt, and the remaining 2 teaspoons sugar in a large bowl. Stir in the flour and whole-wheat flour until blended and smooth.

3 Spray an 8-inch nonstick skillet with nonstick spray and set over medium heat until a drop of water sizzles. Pour in a heaping 2 tablespoons of the batter and swirl to cover the pan. Cook until the underside is set, about 30 seconds. Flip and cook until lightly browned, about 10 seconds longer. Slide the crêpe onto wax paper. Repeat with the remaining batter, making a total of 8 crêpes; stack the crêpes between sheets of wax paper.

4 Place 2 crêpes on a plate; spread each with 2 teaspoons of the ricotta. Top each with 2 tablespoons of the berry mixture. Fold the crêpes closed, then repeat, making a total of 8 filled crêpes. Dust the crêpes evenly with the confectioners' sugar.

PER SERVING (2 filled crêpes): 238 Cal, 4 g Fat, 2 g Sat Fat, 0 g Trans Fat, 64 mg Chol, 240 mg Sod, 39 g Carb, 4 g Fib, 11 g Prot, 199 mg Calc. *POINTS* value: *4.*

EXPRESS LANE For a speedier version of this recipe, forego making the berry mixture and spread 2 teaspoons all-fruit jam in each crêpe instead.

½ **cup** raspberries

½ **cup** blueberries

4 **teaspoons** granulated sugar

1 **teaspoon** fresh lemon juice

1 **large** egg

⅔ **cup** fat-free evaporated milk

1 **teaspoon** unsalted butter, melted

½ **teaspoon** vanilla extract

¼ **teaspoon** salt

½ **cup** all-purpose flour

½ **cup** whole-wheat flour

5 **tablespoons +** 1 **teaspoon** reduced-fat ricotta cheese

2 **teaspoons** confectioners' sugar

Whole-Wheat Banana Waffles

HANDS-ON PREP **10 MIN**
COOK **5 MIN**
SERVES **4**

1 Spray a waffle iron with nonstick spray and heat according to the manufacturer's directions.

2 Place the whole-wheat flour, flour, baking powder, cinnamon, and salt in a food processor or blender; pulse to blend, about 3 seconds. Add the banana, milk, sugar, oil, egg, and vanilla; pulse three times. Scrape down the side of the bowl, then process until smooth, about 30 seconds.

3 Place ½ cup of the batter in the heated waffle iron, close, and cook as directed until brown, about 2 minutes. Repeat with the remaining batter, making a total of 4 waffles.

PER SERVING (1 waffle): 212 Cal, 5 g Fat, 1 g Sat Fat, 0 g Trans Fat, 54 mg Chol, 511 mg Sod, 35 g Carb, 3 g Fib, 7 g Prot, 158 mg Calc. **POINTS** value: **4.**

FOOD NOTE **If you don't have a food processor, you can use a blender. Alternatively, place the dry ingredients in a large bowl. Mash the banana in another bowl and whisk in the remaining wet ingredients. Stir the wet ingredients into the dry ingredients and mix until smooth, about 2 minutes.**

½ **cup whole-wheat flour**

½ **cup all-purpose flour**

1½ **teaspoons baking powder**

½ **teaspoon cinnamon**

½ **teaspoon salt**

1 **ripe banana, peeled and cut into chunks**

½ **cup fat-free milk**

1 **tablespoon sugar**

1 **tablespoon canola oil**

1 **large egg**

1 **teaspoon vanilla extract**

Stuffed French Toast

HANDS-ON PREP **10 MIN**
COOK **10 MIN**
SERVES **6**

1 Spread 2 teaspoons cream cheese on each of three slices of bread, leaving an ⅛-inch border. Spread 2 teaspoons all-fruit spread on each of the three remaining slices of bread, again leaving an ⅛-inch border. Sandwich the slices together, cream cheese to spread, making 3 sandwiches. Cut each sandwich in half.

2 Whisk the egg and egg whites in a large bowl, then whisk in the milk, vanilla, and cinnamon until frothy.

3 Spray a large nonstick skillet with nonstick spray and set over medium heat. Dip 3 of the sandwich halves in the egg mixture, then place in the skillet. Cook 2 minutes, then flip and cook until golden, about 2 minutes longer. Transfer to a plate and repeat with the remaining 3 sandwich halves.

PER SERVING (½ sandwich): 122 Cal, 3 g Fat, 1 g Sat Fat, 0 g Trans Fat, 39 mg Chol, 203 mg Sod, 18 g Carb, 2 g Fib, 6 g Prot, 43 mg Calc. **_POINTS_** value: **_2._**

2 **tablespoons** light cream cheese (Neufchâtel), **softened**

6 **slices** whole-wheat bread

2 **tablespoons** all-fruit spread

1 **large** egg

2 **egg whites**

3 **tablespoons** fat-free milk

1 **teaspoon** vanilla extract

½ **teaspoon** cinnamon

Matzo Brei

HANDS-ON PREP **10 MIN**
COOK **6 MIN**
SERVES **4**

1 Crumble the matzos into a large bowl, pour in the boiling water, and soak for 1 minute. Drain, then stir in apple slices. Let cool, about 5 minutes.

2 Meanwhile, whisk the eggs, egg white, milk, honey, cinnamon, and salt in a medium bowl. Pour the mixture over the soaked matzo and apples; toss well.

3 Spray a 10-inch skillet with nonstick spray and set over medium heat. Add the matzo mixture, gently spreading it over the skillet. Cook for 1 minute, shaking the skillet often to keep the matzo from sticking. Cover the skillet and cook for 4 minutes longer.

4 Uncover the skillet, place a large plate over it, then pick up the skillet, flip it over, and unmold the matzo pancake onto the plate. Return the skillet to the heat and slide the matzo pancake back into the skillet, uncooked side down. Cook until set and slightly browned, about 1 minute. Cut into 4 wedges.

PER SERVING (1 piece): 205 Cal, 3 g Fat, 1 g Sat Fat, 0 g Trans Fat, 106 mg Chol, 202 mg Sod, 37 g Carb, 2 g Fib, 7 g Prot, 43 mg Calc. **POINTS** value: **4.**

GOOD IDEA To really bring out the flavor in this dish, seek out the best honey. Try wildflower, orange blossom, or raspberry. Some gourmet markets stock exotic honey, like acacia, pine tree, or star thistle. Any of these would be delightful in this recipe. Avoid flavored honeys, which masquerade as a natural product—read the label to see if any flavorings or syrups have been added.

4 (6 x 6-inch) squares **whole-wheat matzo**

2 **cups** boiling water

1 **large apple**, peeled, **cored**, and thinly **sliced**

2 **large eggs**

1 **egg white**

¼ **cup** fat-free milk

1 **tablespoon** honey

½ **teaspoon** cinnamon

¼ **teaspoon** salt

Sunday Morning Smoothie

HANDS-ON PREP **5 MIN**
COOK **NONE**
SERVES **4**

Place all the ingredients in a blender. Puree, scraping down the sides of the blender as necessary. Serve at once.

PER SERVING (1 cup): 210 Cal, 1 g Fat, 0 g Sat Fat, 0 g Trans Fat, 1 mg Chol, 53 mg Sod, 44 g Carb, 5 g Fib, 10 g Prot, 157 mg Calc. **POINTS** value: **3.**

1 **very ripe banana,** peeled and cut into thirds

1 **large peach,** halved, pitted, and peeled

4 **ounces** pitted dates (about 5 large dates)

1 **cup** plain fat-free yogurt

½ **teaspoon** vanilla extract

⅛ **teaspoon** cinnamon

⅔ **cup** unsweetened apple juice

¼ **cup** unflavored soy isolate protein powder

2 **tablespoons** wheat germ

1½ **cups** ice cubes (about 8)

Oatmeal Brûlée

HANDS-ON PREP **5 MIN**
COOK **10 MIN**
SERVES **6**

1 Preheat the broiler. Meanwhile, bring the milk to a low simmer in a large saucepan set over medium-high heat.

2 Stir the apricots, currants, and cranberries into the hot milk, then stir in the oats. Cook for 2 minutes, stirring often. Stir in the ginger, cinnamon, nutmeg, and salt. Cook, stirring, until creamy, adjusting the heat so the oatmeal does not stick but the liquid comes to a low simmer, about 3 minutes longer.

3 Spread the cooked cereal into an 8-inch square baking dish or 6 (6-ounce) ramekins. Sprinkle the brown sugar evenly over the top, then broil 5 inches from the heat until the sugar caramelizes, about 30 seconds. Let stand at room temperature about 2 minutes before serving.

PER SERVING (½ cup): 277 Cal, 3 g Fat, 1 g Sat Fat, 0 g Trans Fat, 3 mg Chol, 187 mg Sod, 52 g Carb, 6 g Fib, 12 g Prot, 237 mg Calc. **POINTS** value: **5.**

FOOD NOTE Not all dried cranberries are alike. Read the labels carefully—some are soaked in a sugar solution before being dried; others are coated with a fine mist of corn syrup. For the best taste, choose dried cranberries that contain no additives or preservatives.

- **4 cups** fat-free milk
- **6** dried apricots, chopped into raisin-size pieces
- **¼ cup** dried currants or raisins, chopped
- **¼ cup** dried cranberries
- **3 cups** old-fashioned rolled oats
- **½ teaspoon** ground ginger
- **½ teaspoon** cinnamon
- **¼ teaspoon** grated nutmeg
- **¼ teaspoon** salt
- **1½ tablespoons** packed light brown sugar

Oatmeal Brûlée

Refrigerator Mini Bran Muffins

HANDS-ON PREP **10 MIN**
COOK **10 MIN**
SERVES **36**

1 Preheat the oven to 400°F. Meanwhile, place the bran flakes and wheat bran in a very large bowl; pour in the boiling water, stir, and let stand 3 minutes.

2 Stir in the fruit cocktail, sugar, eggs, buttermilk, oil, baking soda, and salt. Then stir in the flour and whole-wheat flour just until moistened.

3 Spray 24 (1½-inch) mini muffin tins with nonstick spray. Spoon one-third of the batter into the cups, filling each about two-thirds full. Bake the mini muffins until a toothpick inserted in one muffin comes out with a few moist crumbs attached, about 10 minutes. Cover the remaining two-thirds batter tightly and store in the refrigerator for up to 2 weeks.

PER SERVING (2 mini muffins): 76 Cal, 2 g Fat, 0 g Sat Fat, 0 g Trans Fat, 12 mg Chol, 162 mg Sod, 13 g Carb, 2 g Fib, 2 g Prot, 14 mg Calc. **POINTS** value: *1.*

FOOD NOTE This batter makes enough for 72 mini muffins. You can make the batter and store it in the refrigerator for up to 2 weeks and then bake as many muffins as you want at one time. To bake regular-sized muffins, spray standard muffin tins with nonstick spray. Spoon the batter into the cups, filling each about two-thirds full, and bake in a preheated 400°F oven until a toothpick inserted into one muffin comes out with a few moist crumbs attached, about 18 minutes.

2 cups **bran flakes cereal**

1 cup **wheat bran**

1 cup **boiling water**

1 **(15-ounce) can fruit cocktail in light syrup**

½ cup **sugar**

2 large **eggs**

1 cup **low-fat buttermilk**

¼ cup **canola oil**

2 teaspoons **baking soda**

1 teaspoon **salt**

1½ cups **all-purpose flour**

¾ cup **whole-wheat flour**

Pressure-Cooked Sweet Rice Porridge

HANDS-ON PREP **5 MIN**
COOK **15 MIN**
SERVES **8**

1 Place all the ingredients in a pressure cooker, then set it over medium-high heat. Bring to a simmer, stirring all the while so the rice doesn't stick. Lock on the pressure cooker lid according to the manufacturer's directions. Reduce the heat to medium and bring the cooker to high pressure. Cook at high pressure for 6 minutes, adjusting the heat to maintain a constant pressure, as indicated by either the pressure valve or the manufacturer's instructions.

2 Use the quick release method for releasing the pressure. Remove the cooker from the stove and run cold water over it until locking mechanism lets go and pressure subsides. Remove lid and return cooker to medium-high heat.

3 Cook until the rice is creamy but still has some bite and the sauce has thickened, about 1 minute, stirring constantly. Discard the cinnamon stick before serving.

PER SERVING (½ cup): 252 Cal, 1 g Fat, 0 g Sat Fat, 0 g Trans Fat, 2 mg Chol, 141 mg Sod, 54 g Carb, 1 g Fib, 8 g Prot, 171 mg Calc. **POINTS** value: **5.**

FOOD NOTE Use only Arborio rice (a short-grain rice), which holds its toothy texture in this creamy dish, something ordinary long-grain rice will not do. If you don't have a pressure cooker, bring the milk to a simmer in a saucepan over low heat. Place 1 cup of the hot milk and the remaining ingredients in a large saucepan over medium-low heat. Cook, stirring, until the rice is translucent, about 2 minutes. Add ½ cup more milk and cook, stirring, until it is absorbed. Continue to add milk, stirring after each addition until it is absorbed and the rice is just tender. The cooking time from the first addition of milk should be about 30 minutes.

- 4 **cups fat-free milk**
- 1½ **cups Arborio rice**
- 1 **cup raisins**
- 2 **tablespoons** honey
- ¼ **teaspoon** grated nutmeg
- ¼ **teaspoon** salt
- ⅛ **teaspoon ground cloves**
- 1 **cinnamon stick**

Smoked Salmon Pizzas

Smoked Salmon Pizzas

HANDS-ON PREP **5 MIN**
COOK **8 MIN**
SERVES **4**

1 Spray a large nonstick skillet with nonstick spray and set over medium-high heat. Add one lavash and cook, turning occasionally, until crisp and golden, about 4 minutes. Repeat with the remaining lavash. Remove from the heat and let cool slightly.

2 Meanwhile, combine the sour cream, horseradish, salt, and cayenne in a small bowl; spread evenly over each lavash. Top evenly with the tomatoes, onion, smoked salmon, and basil. Cut each lavash in half and serve with a squeeze of lemon.

PER SERVING (½ pizza): 140 Cal, 5 g Fat, 2 g Sat Fat, 0 g Trans Fat, 14 mg Chol, 541 mg Sod, 17 g Carb, 3 g Fib, 9 g Prot, 44 mg Calc. **POINTS** value: **3.**

TRY IT *Lavash* (LAH-vohsh) is a thin round bread that's popular in the Middle East. Look for it in the bread aisle at the supermarket.

2 (10-inch) **whole-wheat lavash breads or flour tortillas**

⅓ **cup light sour cream**

2 **tablespoons prepared horseradish**

¼ **teaspoon salt**

Pinch cayenne

2 **plum tomatoes, diced**

½ **small red onion, thinly sliced**

¼ **pound thinly sliced smoked salmon, cut into strips**

¼ **cup fresh basil leaves**

4 **lemon wedges**

Mesclun Pizza with Pears and Parmesan

HANDS-ON PREP **10 MIN**
COOK **10 MIN**
SERVES **6**

1 Preheat the oven to 450°F. Place the pizza crust on a baking sheet. Bake until lightly browned and crisped, about 7 minutes.

2 Meanwhile, combine the vinegar, oil, garlic, honey, mustard, salt, and pepper in a large bowl. Add the mesclun greens and toss to coat. Spoon the salad over the warm crust, then top with the pear and sprinkle with the cheese. Cut the pizza into 6 wedges and serve at once.

PER SERVING (⅙ of pizza): 203 Cal, 7 g Fat, 2 g Sat Fat, 0 g Trans Fat, 4 mg Chol, 447 mg Sod, 30 g Carb, 2 g Fib, 6 g Prot, 96 mg Calc. *POINTS* value: *4.*

HOW WE DID IT Fresh Parmesan shavings are easy to make: Buy a wedge of Parmesan cheese—for best flavor, seek out authentic Parmigiano-Reggiano cheese; you'll know it by the pale brown rind that has Parmigiano-Reggiano stenciled on it. Using a vegetable peeler, in a downward motion, shave off thin strips from the wedge.

1 (10-ounce) thin prebaked pizza crust

2 tablespoons balsamic vinegar

1 tablespoon olive oil

1 small garlic clove, minced

1 teaspoon honey

1 teaspoon Dijon mustard

¼ teaspoon salt

¼ teaspoon freshly ground pepper

1 (5-ounce) bag mesclun salad greens

1 ripe pear, cored and cut into 12 slices

⅓ cup freshly shaved Parmesan cheese

Microwave Sausage Corn Bread

HANDS-ON PREP **5 MIN**
COOK **10 MIN**
SERVES **6**

1 Combine the flour, cornmeal, baking soda, and salt in a large bowl. Whisk the buttermilk, corn, and egg in a second bowl until well mixed. Add the buttermilk mixture to the flour mixture and stir just until blended. Stir in the chiles and sausage rings.

2 Spray a 10-inch-round, high-sided, microwavable dish with nonstick spray. Spoon the prepared batter into the dish. Microwave on High 4 minutes; cover with plastic wrap, then prick a few holes in the plastic. Continue microwaving on High until firm and cooked through, 4–6 minutes more. (If you don't have a turning table in your microwave, rotate the dish 90 degrees every 2 minutes.) Let stand 3–5 minutes, then cut the corn bread into 6 wedges.

PER SERVING (1 piece): 223 Cal, 3 g Fat, 1 g Sat Fat, 0 g Trans Fat, 42 mg Chol, 834 mg Sod, 40 g Carb, 2 g Fib, 9 g Prot, 59 mg Calc. **POINTS** value: **4.**

FOOD NOTE When using ready-to-eat sausage, be aware that some brands are high in sodium, so check the label. To make this dish in a conventional oven, bake it in a preheated 325°F oven until a toothpick inserted into the center comes out with a few moist crumbs attached, 23 to 25 minutes

1¼ cups **all-purpose flour**

¾ cup **yellow cornmeal**

2 teaspoons **baking soda**

½ teaspoon **salt**

¾ cup + 2 tablespoons **low-fat buttermilk**

½ cup canned **cream-style corn**

1 large **egg**

1 (4½-ounce) can **chopped green chiles, mild or hot**

2 ounces **ready-to-eat turkey breakfast sausage, cut into 1-inch rings**

Dilled Tuna Baguette

HANDS-ON PREP **15 MIN**
COOK **NONE**
SERVES **4**

1 Combine the tuna, cucumber, mayonnaise, onion, dill, capers, and lemon juice with a fork in a bowl until blended.

2 Slice the baguette lengthwise almost all the way through; spread open. Pull out about ½ cup of the bread from the center of both halves, leaving a ½-inch-thick border. (Use the scooped-out bread to make bread crumbs and freeze for another day.) Spoon the tuna mixture into the hollowed-out baguette. Close the baguette, then cut into 4 sandwiches.

PER SERVING (1 sandwich): 276 Cal, 4 g Fat, 1 g Sat Fat, 0 g Trans Fat, 23 mg Chol, 869 mg Sod, 35 g Carb, 4 g Fib, 26 g Prot, 60 mg Calc. **POINTS** value: **5.**

GOOD IDEA If you can't find fresh dill, a few fresh basil leaves, simply placed on top of the tuna mixture, make a tasty alternative.

2 (6-ounce) cans water-packed tuna, drained and flaked

1 cup diced peeled and seeded cucumber

⅓ cup low-fat mayonnaise

¼ cup chopped red onion

¼ cup chopped fresh dill

2 tablespoons capers, drained and chopped

1 tablespoon fresh lemon juice

1 (10-ounce) whole-wheat baguette

Dilled Tuna Baguette

Beef, Pork, and Lamb Entrées

p 55

p 63

p 71

CHAPTER 3

Steak au Poivre

Steak au Poivre

HANDS-ON PREP **5 MIN**
COOK **15 MIN**
SERVES **4**

1 Coat the steaks in the cracked peppercorns. Spray a large nonstick skillet with nonstick spray and set over medium-high heat. Add the steaks and cook, about 4 minutes. Turn the steaks and cook until an instant-read thermometer inserted in the center of the steak registers 145°F for medium-rare, about 3 minutes, or 160°F for medium, about 4 minutes. Transfer the steaks to a plate and cover lightly with foil to keep warm.

2 Add the zucchini and shallots to the skillet; cook, stirring often, until softened, about 3 minutes. Add the brandy and cook about 20 seconds. (If the brandy ignites, cover the skillet with the lid and remove it from the heat until the flame is put out.)

3 Add the broth, then swirl in the mustard and salt until dissolved. Simmer until slightly thickened, about 3 minutes. Serve the sauce with the steaks.

PER SERVING (1 steak with ⅔ cup vegetable sauce): 227 Cal, 8 g Fat, 3 g Sat Fat, 0 g Trans Fat, 65 mg Chol, 521 mg Sod, 5 g Carb, 2 g Fib, 26 g Prot, 43 mg Calc. **POINTS** value: **5.**

HOW WE DID IT To crack the peppercorns, place them in a zip-close plastic bag and crush them with the smooth side of a meat mallet or the bottom of a heavy saucepan. Or crack them in a mortar with a pestle. You want visible shards of peppercorn—not ground, nor even finely crushed.

4 (¼-pound) **filet mignon steaks, or 1 pound beef tenderloin,** trimmed of fat and cut into 4 pieces

1 tablespoon **black peppercorns, cracked**

3 small **zucchini, halved lengthwise, then thinly sliced**

3 **shallots, minced**

3 tablespoons **brandy**

½ **cup reduced-sodium chicken broth**

1 tablespoon **Dijon mustard**

½ **teaspoon salt**

Persian Shish Kebabs

HANDS-ON PREP **10 MIN**
COOK **10 MIN**
SERVES **4**

1 Spray the broiler rack with nonstick spray; preheat the broiler.

2 Meanwhile, combine the broth, pomegranate molasses, salt, and saffron in a small bowl.

3 Skewer the beef and vegetables onto 4 metal skewers, alternating the beef and vegetables. Brush with half the broth mixture.

4 Place the skewers on the broiler rack and broil 5 inches from the heat for 4 minutes. Turn and brush with the remaining broth mixture. Broil until an instant-read thermometer inserted in the beef registers 145°F for medium-rare, about 5 minutes, or 160°F for medium, about 6 minutes. Let stand 1 minute before serving.

PER SERVING (1 skewer): 180 Cal, 4 g Fat, 1 g Sat Fat, 0 g Trans Fat, 60 mg Chol, 672 mg Sod, 12 g Carb, 2 g Fib, 25 g Prot, 25 mg Calc. **POINTS** value: **4.**

HOW WE DID IT We prefer to use metal skewers for this classic dish—they cook the beef from the inside, too, as it broils. If you use wooden skewers, soak them in water for 10 minutes and increase the cooking time by 2 minutes on each side.

¼ **cup reduced-sodium chicken broth**

2 **tablespoons pomegranate molasses or frozen cranberry-juice concentrate, thawed**

1 **teaspoon salt**

½ **teaspoon saffron threads**

1 **pound boneless sirloin steak, trimmed of fat and cut into 1-inch pieces**

4 **large fresh mushrooms, halved**

1 **green bell pepper, seeded and cut into eighths**

1 **red onion, cut into eighths**

1 **zucchini, cut into 8 pieces**

Indonesian Satay

HANDS-ON PREP **5 MIN**
COOK **5 MIN**
SERVES **4**

1 Place 4 (12-inch) bamboo skewers in a large glass of water and soak for 10 minutes. Spray the broiler pan with nonstick spray and preheat the broiler.

2 Grind the cilantro, garlic, water, ginger, and sesame oil in a mini food processor, a spice grinder, or a blender until paste-like. Working in a shallow bowl, rub the paste into the beef strips.

3 Drain the skewers. Thread the beef strips onto them, piercing each strip in at least two places so it will lie flat.

4 Broil 5 inches from the heat, turning once, until cooked through, about 6 minutes. Serve warm or at room temperature.

PER SERVING (1 skewer): 155 Cal, 6 g Fat, 2 g Sat Fat, 0 g Trans Fat, 60 mg Chol, 45 mg Sod, 1 g Carb, 0 g Fib, 23 g Prot, 9 mg Calc. **POINTS** value: **4.**

HOW WE DID IT Cilantro can be quite sandy. To make sure yours has no grit, fill a bowl with cool water, then add the leaves and stir well, allowing the leaves to sit undisturbed for 5 minutes. Carefully skim the leaves off the top, taking care not to disturb any of the sand that has sunk to the bottom. Rinse the cilantro again in a colander, then pat dry in paper towels.

¼ **cup packed** cilantro **leaves**

2 **garlic cloves, quartered**

2 **tablespoons** water

1 **tablespoon minced peeled fresh ginger**

2 **teaspoons** Asian **(dark) sesame oil**

1 **pound** boneless **sirloin steak, trimmed of fat and cut into long ¼-inch-thick strips**

Chinese Beef and Broccoli

HANDS-ON PREP **10 MIN**
COOK **5 MIN**
SERVES **4**

1 Spray a large nonstick wok or high-sided skillet with nonstick spray and set over high heat until a drop of water sizzles. Add the scallions, garlic, ginger, and orange zest; stir-fry until softened and fragrant, about 1 minute.

2 Add the beef strips and stir-fry until browned, about 3 minutes. Add the broccoli and stir-fry 2 minutes. Sir in the soy sauce and orange juice; bring to a simmer and cook 20 seconds.

3 Combine the cornstarch and water in a small bowl until smooth. Add the cornstarch mixture to the wok and cook, stirring constantly, until thickened, about 30 seconds.

PER SERVING (1 cup): 132 Cal, 3 g Fat, 1 g Sat Fat, 0 g Trans Fat, 45 mg Chol, 316 mg Sod, 7 g Carb, 2 g Fib, 19 g Prot, 45 mg Calc. **POINTS** value: **2.**

HOW WE DID IT The zest is the very top layer of a citrus fruit, just the brightly colored skin, not the bitter, white pith underneath. To remove the zest, use a citrus zester, a box grater, or a microplane. In all cases, do not press down—lightly run the tool along the outer surface of the fruit, just until the brightly colored skin comes off. Serve over rice (½ cup cooked rice will increase the per-serving **POINTS** value by 2).

3 **scallions**, thinly sliced

2 **garlic cloves**, minced

1 **tablespoon minced peeled fresh ginger**

1 **tablespoon grated orange zest**

¾ **pound boneless sirloin steak**, trimmed of fat and cut into 2 x ¼-inch strips

3 **cups fresh broccoli florets**, or **frozen broccoli florets**, thawed

2 **tablespoons** reduced-sodium soy sauce

2 **tablespoons** fresh orange juice

1 **teaspoon** cornstarch

1 **tablespoon** cold water

Chinese Beef and Broccoli

Beef Orzo Soup

HANDS-ON PREP **5 MIN**
COOK **15 MIN**
SERVES **4**

1 Spray a large nonstick saucepan with nonstick spray and set over medium heat. Add the onion and cook, stirring, until translucent, about 3 minutes.

2 Add the ground beef and cook, breaking it apart with a wooden spoon, until browned, about 3 minutes.

3 Add the mushrooms and cook, stirring occasionally, until softened, about 3 minutes. Add the thyme and sage; cook until fragrant, about 20 seconds. Add the broth, stirring to scrape up any browned bits from the bottom of the pan. Stir in the orzo, Swiss chard, salt, and pepper; bring to a boil. Reduce the heat, and simmer, covered, about 8 minutes.

PER SERVING (1½ cups): 291 Cal, 7 g Fat, 2 g Sat Fat, 0 g Trans Fat, 48 mg Chol, 726 mg Sod, 31 g Carb, 5 g Fib, 28 g Prot, 104 mg Calc. **POINTS** value: **6.**

EXPRESS LANE **To save time, buy the mushrooms already sliced in a package.**

1 onion, chopped

¾ pound ground lean beef (5% or less fat)

3 cups thinly sliced fresh white or cremini mushrooms

1½ teaspoons dried thyme

1 teaspoon dried rubbed sage

4 cups reduced-sodium beef broth

¾ cup orzo

1 bunch Swiss chard, stemmed and chopped

½ teaspoon salt

Freshly ground pepper

Korean Lettuce Rolls

HANDS-ON PREP **10 MIN**
COOK **5 MIN**
SERVES **4**

1 Mix the ground beef, garlic, sherry, soy sauce, red chile sauce, brown sugar, and ginger in a medium bowl until well combined.

2 Spray a large nonstick skillet with nonstick spray and set over medium heat. Add the beef mixture and cook, breaking it apart with a wooden spoon, until cooked through, about 3 minutes. Stir in the sesame oil.

3 To serve, place ¼ cup cooked ground beef mixture in each of the lettuce-leaf cups. Top each with one-eighth of the sliced cucumber and sliced bell pepper. Serve at once.

PER SERVING (2 filled lettuce cups): 195 Cal, 7 g Fat, 3 g Sat Fat, 0 g Trans Fat, 64 mg Chol, 228 mg Sod, 8 g Carb, 1 g Fib, 23 g Prot, 29 mg Calc. **POINTS** value: **4.**

GOOD IDEA For an even spicier dish, serve bottled Asian red chile sauce on the side and splash a few drops on each roll.

1 **pound** ground lean beef **(5% or less fat)**

4 **garlic cloves,** minced

1 **tablespoon** sherry **or dry vermouth**

1 **tablespoon** reduced-sodium soy sauce

2 **teaspoons** bottled **Asian red chile sauce**

2 **teaspoons packed light brown sugar**

1 **teaspoon** ground **ginger**

1 **teaspoon** Asian (dark) **sesame oil**

8 **iceberg lettuce leaves**

1 **cucumber, peeled and thinly sliced**

1 **red bell pepper, seeded and thinly sliced**

Mushroom Burgers with
Spiced Ketchup

Mushroom Burgers with Spiced Ketchup

HANDS-ON PREP **5 MIN**
COOK **10 MIN**
SERVES **4**

1 Place the dried mushrooms and sliced mushrooms in a food processor fitted with the chopping blade or a blender; pulse until finely ground. Transfer to a medium bowl and combine with the beef, parsley, tarragon, salt, onion powder, and pepper. Shape into 4 burgers.

2 Spray a large nonstick skillet with nonstick spray and set over medium-high heat. Add the burgers and cook, turning once, until an instant-read thermometer inserted in the side of a burger registers 160°F, about 8 minutes.

3 Meanwhile, mix the ketchup, allspice, cloves, and garlic powder in a small bowl until smooth. Serve the burgers with the spiced ketchup on the side.

PER SERVING (1 burger patty with scant 2 teaspoons spiced ketchup): 187 Cal, 6 g Fat, 3 g Sat Fat, 0 g Trans Fat, 64 mg Chol, 735 mg Sod, 10 g Carb, 2 g Fib, 23 g Prot, 25 mg Calc.
POINTS value: *4.*

EXPRESS LANE If you want to get a jump start on a busy weeknight meal, the uncooked burgers can be made in advance. Store the patties, tightly covered, in the refrigerator for up to 24 hours—the mushroom flavor will become even more intense. Dried mushrooms are available in the produce section of most supermarkets. Sauté ¼ pound sliced fresh mushrooms in 2 teaspoons olive oil to serve with the burgers and up the per-serving *POINTS* value by ½.

1 **ounce dried porcini, chanterelle, or black trumpet mushrooms**

5 **large fresh white or cremini mushrooms, sliced**

1 **pound ground lean beef (5% or less fat)**

2 **teaspoons dried parsley**

1½ **teaspoons dried tarragon**

1 **teaspoon salt**

½ **teaspoon onion powder**

Freshly ground pepper

2 **tablespoons ketchup**

½ **teaspoon ground allspice**

¼ **teaspoon ground cloves**

⅛ **teaspoon garlic powder**

Microwave Stuffed Tomatoes

HANDS-ON PREP **8 MIN**
COOK **12 MIN**
SERVES **4**

1 Cut ¼-inch slices from the tops of the tomatoes. Using a small spoon, carefully hollow out the tomatoes, keeping the tomato shells intact. Save the tops and scooped-out pulp for soups, stews etc.

2 Spray a large nonstick skillet with nonstick spray and set over medium-high heat. Add the onion and cook, stirring, until translucent, about 2 minutes. Add the garlic and cook, stirring until fragrant, about 20 seconds. Add the ground beef and cook, breaking it apart with a wooden spoon, until browned, about 2 minutes.

3 Stir in the beans, chili powder, cumin, and salt; cook, stirring, until fragrant, about 20 seconds. Remove the skillet from the heat and stir in the water.

4 Spoon ½ cup of the beef mixture into each of the tomatoes. Sprinkle each stuffed tomato with 1 tablespoon cheese. Place the stuffed tomatoes in a microwavable dish; microwave on High until heated through, the tomatoes have softened somewhat, and the cheese has melted, about 6 minutes. Let stand 1 minute at room temperature before serving.

PER SERVING (1 stuffed tomato): 204 Cal, 4 g Fat, 2 g Sat Fat, 0 g Trans Fat, 34 mg Chol, 634 mg Sod, 24 g Carb, 6 g Fib, 18 g Prot, 112 mg Calc. **POINTS** value: **4.**

HOW WE DID IT Cook the tomatoes in a microwavable baking dish just large enough to hold them securely in place, so the tomatoes don't collapse at the sides while they heat.

- **4 large tomatoes**
- **1 small onion, chopped**
- **2 garlic cloves, minced**
- **½ pound ground lean beef (5% or less fat)**
- **1 cup canned black beans, rinsed and drained**
- **1½ tablespoons chili powder**
- **1 teaspoon ground cumin**
- **½ teaspoon salt**
- **¼ cup water**
- **4 tablespoons shredded fat-free cheddar cheese**

Beef Fried Rice

HANDS-ON PREP **5 MIN**
COOK **10 MIN**
SERVES **4**

1 Spray a large nonstick wok or high-sided nonstick skillet with nonstick spray and set over high heat. Add the scallions, ginger, and garlic; stir-fry until softened, about 1 minute. Add the ground beef and cook, breaking it apart with a wooden spoon, until browned, about 3 minutes.

2 Add the five-spice powder and cook until fragrant, 20 seconds. Add the mixed vegetables and stir-fry 2 minutes.

3 Add the brown rice and stir-fry 2 minutes. Stir in the soy sauce, hoisin sauce, and chile sauce. Stir-fry until heated through, about 1 minute.

PER SERVING (1¼ cups): 226 Cal, 4 g Fat, 2 g Sat Fat, 0 g Trans Fat, 32 mg Chol, 688 mg Sod, 31 g Carb, 6 g Fib, 16 g Prot, 52 mg Calc. *POINTS* value: *4.*

FOOD NOTE Five-spice powder is a blend of ground cinnamon, star anise, fennel, ginger, and cloves. Because of the interaction of the oils in the ground spices, five-spice powder has a short shelf life, so, after opening, store it for no more than 3 months on the shelf or 6 months in the freezer.

---

3 **scallions**, thinly sliced

1 tablespoon minced **peeled fresh ginger**

2 **garlic cloves**, minced

½ **pound** ground lean **beef (5% or less fat)**

1 teaspoon **five-spice powder**

1 (10-ounce) box **frozen mixed vegetables, preferably an Asian mixture, thawed**

2 **cups** cooked **brown rice**

1 tablespoon **reduced-sodium soy sauce**

2 teaspoons **hoisin sauce or oyster sauce**

2 teaspoons **bottled Asian red chile sauce**

Seven-Layer Salad

HANDS-ON PREP **15 MIN**
COOK **5 MIN**
SERVES **4**

1 Spray a large nonstick skillet with nonstick spray and set over medium heat. Add the ground beef and cook, breaking it apart with a wooden spoon, until cooked through, about 3 minutes.

2 Add the chili powder, cumin, cinnamon, salt, and pepper. Cook until fragrant, about 20 seconds; set aside.

3 Layer the lettuce, tomatoes, beans, jicama, and scallions in a large glass salad bowl or a large round casserole dish. Top with the warm ground beef mixture.

4 Mix the salsa, sour cream, and lime juice in a small bowl. Spoon this mixture over the top of the salad, spreading to cover. Serve at once.

PER SERVING (1½ cups): 282 Cal, 6 g Fat, 2 g Sat Fat, 0 g Trans Fat, 50 mg Chol, 758 mg Sod, 36 g Carb, 12 g Fib, 24 g Prot, 140 mg Calc. *POINTS* value: **5.**

EXPRESS LANE The salad can be made in advance if you want to plan ahead for a instant meal: Cook the beef and spices; store, covered, in the refrigerator for up to 24 hours. Layer the vegetables in the bowl and mix together the sour cream topping; store these separately, covered, in the refrigerator. Microwave the cooked ground beef on High until it reaches room temperature, about 1 minute, then build the salad as directed above.

¾ **pound** ground lean beef (5% or less fat)

2 **teaspoons** chili powder

1 **teaspoon** ground cumin

½ **teaspoon** cinnamon

½ **teaspoon** salt

Freshly ground pepper

4 cups shredded romaine lettuce (about ½ head)

2 large tomatoes, diced

1 cup canned pinto beans, rinsed and drained

1 small jicama, peeled and cut into matchstick-thin strips

3 scallions, thinly sliced

1 cup bottled fat-free salsa

½ cup fat-free sour cream

2 teaspoons fresh lime juice

Seven-Layer Salad

Cranberry Pork Tenderloin with Squash Puree

HANDS-ON PREP **5 MIN**
COOK **15 MIN**
SERVES **4**

1 Spray a large nonstick skillet with nonstick spray and set over medium-high heat. Sprinkle the pork with ½ teaspoon of the salt and the pepper. Add to the skillet and cook until browned, about 2 minutes on each side. Transfer the pork to a plate.

2 Add the broth to the skillet, scraping up any browned bits from the bottom of the pan. Add the cranberry sauce, orange zest, and the pork and any accumulated juices; bring the mixture to a simmer. Reduce the heat, cover, and simmer until the pork is cooked through, about 10 minutes. Stir in the vinegar.

3 Meanwhile, combine the squash puree, cinnamon, nutmeg, and the remaining ½ teaspoon salt in a microwavable bowl. Dot with the butter. Microwave on High for 30 seconds. Stir, then microwave, stirring twice more, until heated through, 2–3 minutes.

4 To serve, divide the squash puree among 4 plates; top with the pork and sauce.

PER SERVING (2 pieces pork, 2 tablespoons sauce, and ¼ cup squash puree): 264 Cal, 8 g Fat, 3 g Sat Fat, 0 g Trans Fat, 95 mg Chol, 728 mg Sod, 14 g Carb, 3 g Fib, 33 g Prot, 28 mg Calc. **POINTS** value: **5.**

HOW WE DID IT Pork tenderloins often have a thin, translucent, but tough covering, called the "silver skin" for both its look and feel. Remove it by slipping a sharp knife just under one end of the silver skin, then gently cutting underneath it and pulling it off. Do not cut into the meat—simply remove this outer layer. Or ask your butcher to do it for you.

1 (1¼-pound) **pork tenderloin,** trimmed of fat and cut into 8 medallions (about 1½ inches thick)

1 teaspoon **salt**

Freshly ground **pepper**

½ cup **reduced-sodium chicken broth**

¼ cup **whole-berry cranberry sauce**

1 tablespoon **grated orange zest**

1 teaspoon **balsamic vinegar**

1 (10-ounce) **box frozen winter squash puree,** thawed

½ teaspoon **cinnamon**

¼ teaspoon **ground nutmeg**

2 teaspoons **unsalted butter**

Easy Pork Sauté

HANDS-ON PREP **5 MIN**
COOK **15 MIN**
SERVES **4**

1 Place the pork chops between sheets of wax paper. Pound them to ¼-inch thickness using the smooth side of a meat mallet or the bottom of a heavy, large saucepan. Season the chops with the salt and pepper; set aside.

2 Toast the walnut pieces in a 12-inch nonstick skillet set over medium heat, stirring often, about 4 minutes. Transfer the walnuts to a plate and set aside.

3 Spray the skillet with nonstick spray and return it to medium heat. Add the pork chops and cook until brown and cooked through, about 2 minutes on each side. Transfer them to the plate with the walnuts.

4 Add the broccoli and wine to the skillet; cover and steam until crisp-tender, about 5 minutes. Add the grapefruit sections and the pork, walnuts, and any accumulated juices to the skillet. Cook until heated through, about 1 minute.

PER SERVING (1 chop with ½ cup vegetables and sauce): 256 Cal, 12 g Fat, 3 g Sat Fat, 0 g Trans Fat, 70 mg Chol, 642 mg Sod, 10 g Carb, 2 g Fib, 27 g Prot, 40 mg Calc. **POINTS** value: **6.**

HOW WE DID IT To section the grapefruit, cut it in half crosswise. Use a grapefruit spoon to release the small sections from the fruit, as you would if you were eating it for breakfast, taking care to keep the sections intact as you remove them.

4 (¼-pound) boneless pork loin chops, trimmed of fat

1 teaspoon salt

Freshly ground pepper, to taste

3 tablespoons walnut pieces

2 cups fresh broccoli florets, or frozen florets, thawed

¼ cup dry white wine or dry vermouth

1 large grapefruit, sectioned

Pork Noodle Soup

Pork Noodle Soup

1 Bring 2 quarts water to a boil in a large covered pot set over high heat. Add the noodles, reduce the heat, and cook until tender, about 10 minutes.

2 Meanwhile, bring the broth, water, vegetables, pork, and ginger to a simmer in a large saucepan set over high heat. Reduce the heat and simmer 10 minutes.

3 Drain the noodles, then add them to the soup along with the vinegar. Stir well before serving.

PER SERVING (2 cups): 225 Cal, 2 g Fat, 1 g Sat Fat, 0 g Trans Fat, 27 mg Chol, 1158 mg Sod, 38 g Carb, 5 g Fib, 17 g Prot, 44 mg Calc. **POINTS** value: **4.**

TRY IT *Udon* (oo-DOHN) are thick Japanese noodles. Look for them in the Asian aisle of your supermarket, or use spaghetti.

6 ounces **udon noodles**

4 cups **vegetable broth**

2 cups **water**

1 (8-ounce) **box frozen mixed Chinese vegetables (snow peas, water chestnuts, red bell pepper, mushrooms), thawed**

6 ounces **pork tenderloin, trimmed of fat and cut into matchstick-thin strips**

1 teaspoon **ground ginger**

1 teaspoon **rice vinegar**

Pork Paprikash

HANDS-ON PREP **5 MIN**
COOK **10 MIN**
SERVES **4**

1 Place the pork chops between sheets of wax paper. Pound them to ¼-inch thickness using the smooth side of a meat mallet or the bottom of a heavy, large saucepan. Season the chops with the salt and pepper.

2 Spray a large nonstick skillet with nonstick spray and set over medium-high heat. Add the pork chops and cook until browned and cooked through, about 2 minutes on each side. Transfer to a plate and cover with foil to keep warm.

3 Stir the broth into the skillet, scraping up any browned bits from the bottom of the pan. Stir in the onion powder and garlic powder, then add the chard. Reduce the heat, cover, and simmer about 5 minutes.

4 Stir in the paprika; cook, uncovered, 20 seconds. Stir in the sour cream and heat 10 seconds; do not allow the sauce to boil. Slip the pork chops and any accumulated juices into the sauce. Cover the skillet and set aside off the heat for 5 minutes before serving.

PER SERVING (1 chop with ½ cup sauce and greens): 224 Cal, 9 g Fat, 3 g Sat Fat, 0 g Trans Fat, 70 mg Chol, 664 mg Sod, 9 g Carb, 4 g Fib, 28 g Prot, 95 mg Calc. *POINTS* value: *4.*

GOOD IDEA For an extra kick of flavor, you can substitute hot Hungarian paprika for up to half of the mild paprika in this dish, if you like.

4 (¼-pound) boneless pork loin chops, trimmed of fat

½ teaspoon salt

Freshly ground pepper

¾ cup reduced-sodium chicken broth

½ teaspoon onion powder

¼ teaspoon garlic powder

2 bunches Swiss chard, stemmed and chopped

2 tablespoons paprika

2 tablespoons fat-free sour cream

Cellophane Noodles and Pork

HANDS-ON PREP **10 MIN**
COOK **10 MIN**
SERVES **4**

1 Place the cellophane noodles in a large bowl; cover them with hot water. Set aside to soak until softened, about 10 minutes.

2 Meanwhile, spray a large nonstick wok or high-sided skillet with nonstick spray and set over medium-high heat until a drop of water sizzles. Add the pork and stir-fry, breaking it apart with a wooden spoon, until browned, about 3 minutes.

3 Add the scallions, ginger, and garlic; stir-fry until fragrant, about 25 seconds. Stir in the soy sauce, vinegar, sesame oil, and chile sauce. Then pour in the broth, scraping up any browned bits from the bottom of the wok. Bring the mixture to a simmer.

4 Drain the noodles and stir into the simmering sauce in the wok. Reduce the heat and simmer until the liquid is absorbed into the noodles, about 3 minutes.

PER SERVING (¾ cup): 185 Cal, 5 g Fat, 1 g Sat Fat, 0 g Trans Fat, 27 mg Chol, 366 mg Sod, 24 g Carb, 2 g Fib, 12 g Prot, 29 mg Calc. **POINTS** value: **4.**

FOOD NOTE If you are lucky enough to live near an Asian market, you may be able to find fresh cellophane noodles (sometimes called bean-thread noodles). If you are using the fresh, don't soak them at all; simply toss them into the dish as you would the soaked noodles.

¼ **pound** dry cellophane noodles

6 **ounces** ground lean pork

6 **scallions, thinly sliced**

2 **tablespoons minced** peeled fresh ginger

2 **garlic cloves,** minced

2 **tablespoons** reduced-sodium soy sauce

2 **tablespoons** rice vinegar

1 **teaspoon** Asian (dark) sesame oil

1 **teaspoon** bottled Asian red chile sauce, or ½ **teaspoon** crushed red pepper

⅓ **cup** reduced-sodium chicken broth

Oven-Fried Pork Chops

HANDS-ON PREP **5 MIN**
COOK **15 MIN**
SERVES **4**

1 Preheat the oven to 500°F. Spray a large rimmed baking sheet with nonstick spray.

2 Combine the bread crumbs, paprika, fennel seeds, celery seeds, onion powder, salt, garlic powder, and pepper on a piece of wax paper; set aside.

3 Place the pork chops between sheets of wax paper. Pound them to ¼-inch thickness using the smooth side of a meat mallet or the bottom of a heavy, large saucepan.

4 Place the buttermilk in a shallow bowl. Dip the chops in the buttermilk, then coat both sides with the bread crumb mixture. Place the chops on the prepared baking sheet and put in the preheating oven. Bake until browned and cooked through, about 12 minutes.

PER SERVING (1 chop): 218 Cal, 9 g Fat, 3 g Sat Fat, 0 g Trans Fat, 71 mg Chol, 403 mg Sod, 6 g Carb, 2 g Fib, 26 g Prot, 64 mg Calc. **POINTS** value: **5.**

EXPRESS LANE To make cleanup a snap, coat the baking sheet with foil, then spray the foil with nonstick spray. Or forego the nonstick spray altogether and coat the baking sheet with nonstick foil. Serve the chops with a quick skillet sauté of sliced zucchini and yellow bell pepper strips.

½ **cup** fresh whole-wheat bread crumbs

1 **tablespoon** paprika

2 **teaspoons** fennel seeds

½ **teaspoon** celery seeds

½ **teaspoon** onion powder

½ **teaspoon** salt

¼ **teaspoon** garlic powder

Freshly ground pepper

4 (¼-pound) boneless pork loin chops, trimmed of fat

½ **cup** low-fat buttermilk

Oven-Fried Pork Chops

Salade aux Lardons

HANDS-ON PREP **5 MIN**
COOK **15 MIN**
SERVES **4**

1 Bring a large skillet half-filled with water to a boil over high heat.

2 Meanwhile, spray a large nonstick skillet with nonstick spray and set over medium heat. Add the Canadian bacon and cook, stirring, until browned, about 4 minutes. Transfer the bacon to a plate lined with paper towels. Toss the bacon and the greens together in a large bowl.

3 When the water is boiling in the skillet, add 2 teaspoons vinegar. Crack the eggs into the skillet and reduce the heat. Poach the eggs until the whites are set but the yolks are still runny, about 2 minutes. Use a slotted spoon to transfer them gently to a second plate lined with paper towels.

4 Add the olive oil to the skillet that held the bacon and return it to medium heat. Add the shallots and cook, stirring, until softened, about 2 minutes. Add the broth and bring to a simmer, scraping up any browned bits from the bottom of the skillet. Boil until the liquid is reduced to a glaze, about 20 seconds. Stir in the remaining 2 tablespoons vinegar, the mustard, tarragon, salt, and pepper. Pour this mixture over the greens and Canadian bacon; toss well.

5 To serve, divide the greens among 4 plates. Top each salad with a poached egg and serve at once.

PER SERVING (2 cups dressed greens and 1 poached egg): 220 Cal, 13 g Fat, 3 g Sat Fat, 0 g Trans Fat, 239 mg Chol, 1055 mg Sod, 6 g Carb, 3 g Fib, 20 g Prot, 100 mg Calc. *POINTS* value: *5.*

HOW WE DID IT To bring the water to a boil as quickly as possible in Step 1, cover the skillet with a lid or piece of foil.

- ½ **pound** Canadian **bacon, diced**
- 8 **cups packaged mixed greens, preferably a mix that includes frisée and radicchio**
- 2 **tablespoons + 2 teaspoons** white-**wine vinegar or Champagne vinegar**
- 4 **large eggs**
- 1 **tablespoon** olive oil
- 2 **medium shallots, minced**
- ¼ **cup reduced-sodium chicken broth**
- 2 **teaspoons** Dijon **mustard**
- 1 **teaspoon dried tarragon**
- ¼ **teaspoon** salt
- **Freshly ground pepper**

Grilled Lamb Chops with Mint-Pecan Pesto

HANDS-ON PREP **10 MIN**
COOK **10 MIN**
SERVES **4**

1 Spray the broiler rack with nonstick spray. Preheat the broiler.

2 Mix the lemon zest, 1 teaspoon of the lemon juice, 2 of the minced garlic cloves, ½ teaspoon of the salt, and the pepper in a small bowl until the mixture forms a paste. Rub this paste on both sides of the chops.

3 Place the chops on the broiler rack and broil 5 inches from the heat, until an instant-read thermometer inserted in the center of the chops registers 145°F for medium-rare, about 5 minutes on each side.

4 Meanwhile, prepare the pesto by placing the mint, parsley, water, chopped pecan pieces, the remaining minced garlic clove, 1 teaspoon lemon juice, and ¼ teaspoon salt in a food processor fitted with the chopping blade, a spice grinder, or a mini food processor; process until smooth. Serve with the chops.

PER SERVING (1 chop and 1½ tablespoons pesto): 159 Cal, 10 g Fat, 3 g Sat Fat, 1 g Trans Fat, 50 mg Chol, 492 mg Sod, 2 g Carb, 1 g Fib, 16 g Prot, 35 mg Calc. **POINTS** value: **4.**

HOW WE DID IT If you find rib chops, you should buy so-called "double chops" (chops with two bones, or the meat from two with only one bone still attached). They're about 1½ inches thick.

2 teaspoon grated lemon zest

2 teaspoons fresh lemon juice

3 garlic cloves, minced

¾ teaspoon salt

Freshly ground pepper

4 (6-ounce) rib or loin bone-in lamb chops, trimmed of fat

½ cup packed fresh mint leaves

¼ cup packed flat-leaf parsley leaves

3 tablespoons water

1½ tablespoons chopped pecans

Roast Rack of Lamb
with Belgian Endive

Roast Rack of Lamb with Belgian Endive

HANDS-ON PREP **5 MIN**
COOK **15 MIN**
SERVES **4**

1 Adjust the racks to divide the oven into thirds. Preheat the oven to 550°F.

2 Spray a shallow roasting pan with nonstick spray. Split each endive into 6 wedges, cutting through the core; place in the roasting pan. Place the pan on the top rack of the preheating oven. Bake until tender, about 15 minutes.

3 Meanwhile, place a heavy ovenproof skillet, preferably cast-iron, over medium-high heat. Mix the rosemary, thyme, lemon zest, garlic powder, salt, and pepper in a small bowl. Rub this mixture into the lamb. Place the rack of lamb, bones curving up, in the hot skillet. Brown 2 minutes, turn, and add the cherry tomatoes. Place the skillet on the bottom rack of the still preheating oven.

4 Roast until an instant-read thermometer inserted in the thickest part of the lamb registers 145°F for medium-rare, about 12 minutes. Let the lamb stand at room temperature 1 minute before carving between the bones and serving.

PER SERVING (2 chops with 3 tomatoes and 3 endive wedges): 115 Cal, 6 g Fat, 2 g Sat Fat, 0 g Trans Fat, 34 mg Chol, 341 mg Sod, 5 g Carb, 3 g Fib, 11 g Prot, 52 mg Calc. **POINTS** value: **2.**

HOW WE DID IT To get this dish from oven to table in 20 minutes, follow this strategy: As soon as you've got the endive prepared, pop them in the oven after it has been preheating about 2 minutes, and as soon as you've browned the lamb, put it in the oven, after it has been preheating for about 7 minutes.

- 2 **Belgian endive**
- 2 **teaspoons** dried **rosemary, crumbled**
- 2 **teaspoon** dried **thyme**
- 2 **teaspoons grated lemon zest**
- 1 **teaspoon** garlic **powder**
- ½ **teaspoon salt**

Freshly ground pepper

- 1 **(1¼-pound) 8-bone rack of lamb loin, trimmed of fat and Frenched**
- 12 **cherry tomatoes**

Pressure Cooker Lamb Tagine

HANDS-ON PREP **8 MIN**
COOK **12 MIN**
SERVES **4**

1 Spray a pressure cooker with nonstick spray and set it over medium-high heat. Add the onion and garlic, cook, stirring, until softened, about 2 minutes. Add the lamb and cook, stirring, just until lightly browned, about 2 minutes.

2 Stir in the cinnamon, cumin, turmeric, ginger, salt, and pepper; cook until fragrant, about 20 seconds. Stir in the broth, dried apricots, carrots, and potato.

3 Lock the lid in place and raise the heat to high. Bring the cooker to high pressure, following the manufacturer's directions. Reduce the heat and cook at high pressure for 8 minutes.

4 Place the pot in the sink and run cold water over it to bring the pressure down quickly. When the pressure indicator releases, remove the pot from the sink and unlock the lid, following the manufacturer's directions. Stir in the mint, lemon zest, and lemon juice just before serving.

PER SERVING (1 cup): 267 Cal, 8 g Fat, 3 g Sat Fat, 1 g Trans Fat, 78 mg Chol, 580 mg Sod, 21 g Carb, 4 g Fib, 27 g Prot, 63 mg Calc. **POINTS** value: **5.**

FOOD NOTE If you don't have a pressure cooker, heat the oven to 400°F. Brown the ingredients in a Dutch oven as above. Add the remaining ingredients, cover, and bake until the lamb and vegetables are tender, about 1 hour and 20 minutes. Stir in the mint, lemon zest, and lemon juice.

1 large onion, thinly sliced

2 garlic cloves, minced

1 pound lean lamb leg, trimmed of fat and cut into ½-inch pieces

1½ teaspoons cinnamon

1½ teaspoons ground cumin

1 teaspoon turmeric

1 teaspoon ground ginger

½ teaspoon salt

¼ teaspoon ground pepper

1½ cups reduced-sodium chicken broth

12 dried apricot halves

1 cup bagged shredded carrots

1 cup bagged diced potato

1 tablespoon chopped fresh mint

2 teaspoons grated lemon zest

1 teaspoon fresh lemon juice

Pasta Moussaka

HANDS-ON PREP **5 MIN**
COOK **15 MIN**
SERVES **6**

1 Bring 3 quarts of water to a boil in a large saucepan over high heat.

2 Meanwhile, spray a medium saucepan with nonstick spray and set over medium-high heat. Add the onion and cook, stirring, until translucent, about 2 minutes. Add the garlic and cook, stirring, until fragrant, about 20 seconds.

3 Add the ground lamb and cook, breaking it apart with a wooden spoon, until cooked through, about 2 minutes. Add the oregano, cinnamon, nutmeg, salt, and pepper; cook until fragrant, about 15 seconds. Stir in the broth, parsley, wine, and tomato paste; bring to a boil. Reduce the heat and simmer, covered, stirring occasionally, about 10 minutes.

4 Meanwhile, add the pasta to the boiling water and cook until al dente, about 2 minutes. Drain, rinse with warm water, and serve with the sauce and Parmesan cheese.

PER SERVING (½ cup sauce, ½ cup pasta, and 1 teaspoon Parmesan cheese): 308 Cal, 8 g Fat, 2 g Sat Fat, 0 g Trans Fat, 94 mg Chol, 374 mg Sod, 35 g Carb, 3 g Fib, 24 g Prot, 56 mg Calc. **_POINTS_** value: **_6._**

1 large onion, **chopped**

2 garlic cloves, **minced**

1 **pound** ground lean lamb

2 **teaspoons** dried oregano

1 **teaspoon** cinnamon

½ **teaspoon** grated nutmeg

½ **teaspoon** salt

¼ **teaspoon** ground pepper

½ **cup** reduced-sodium chicken broth

⅓ **cup** packed flat-leaf parsley leaves, **chopped**

¼ **cup** dry white wine **or** dry vermouth

3 **tablespoons** tomato paste

¾ **pound** fresh linguine or fettuccine

2 **tablespoons** grated Parmesan cheese

Easy Poultry Dinners

p 86

p 92

p 112

CHAPTER 4

Chicken with Wild Mushroom–Marsala Sauce

HANDS-ON PREP **5 MIN**
COOK **15 MIN**
SERVES **4**

1 Sprinkle the chicken with the salt and pepper. Heat 1 teaspoon of the oil in a large nonstick skillet over medium-high heat. Add the chicken and cook until lightly browned, about 3 minutes on each side. Transfer the chicken to a plate.

2 Add the remaining 1 teaspoon oil to the same skillet, then add the mushrooms; cook over medium-high heat, stirring often, until the mushrooms are browned, about 4 minutes.

3 Whisk the Marsala, broth, and flour in a small bowl until blended. Pour into the skillet along with the garlic. Cook, stirring constantly, until the mixture bubbles and thickens, about 1 minute. Return the chicken to the skillet, turn to coat with the sauce, and sprinkle with the thyme. Reduce the heat and simmer, covered, turning the chicken occasionally, until the chicken is cooked through, about 5 minutes.

PER SERVING (1 piece chicken and generous ⅓ cup sauce): 237 Cal, 7 g Fat, 2 g Sat Fat, 0 g Trans Fat, 86 mg Chol, 423 mg Sod, 7 g Carb, 1 g Fib, 34 g Prot, 28 mg Calc. **POINTS** value: **5.**

FOOD NOTE If you are unable to find mushrooms already sliced and opt for whole shiitakes, be sure to remove the stems, which are very tough.

- **4 (5-ounce)** skinless, boneless chicken breast halves
- **½ teaspoon** salt
- **¼ teaspoon** freshly ground pepper
- **2 teaspoons** olive oil
- **3 (4-ounce)** packages sliced assorted fresh wild mushrooms (such as oyster, baby bella, and shiitake)
- **⅓ cup** dry Marsala wine
- **⅓ cup** reduced-sodium chicken broth
- **2 teaspoons** all-purpose flour
- **2** garlic cloves, minced
- **2 teaspoons** chopped fresh thyme, or ½ teaspoon dried

Chicken Cutlets Milanese

HANDS-ON PREP **10 MIN**
COOK **5 MIN**
SERVES **4**

1 Mix the bread crumbs and Parmesan cheese on a sheet of wax paper; coat the chicken in the mixture. Heat the oil in a large nonstick skillet over medium heat. Add the chicken and cook until browned and cooked through, about 2½ minutes on each side.

2 Meanwhile, combine the arugula, tomato, and onion in a medium bowl. Add the dressing and toss to coat.

3 Place one piece of chicken on each of 4 serving plates. Top each of the cutlets with ¾ cup arugula salad and ground pepper to taste.

PER SERVING (1 piece chicken and ¾ cup salad): 197 Cal, 8 g Fat, 2 g Sat Fat, 0 g Trans Fat, 54 mg Chol, 312 mg Sod, 9 g Carb, 1 g Fib, 22 g Prot, 96 mg Calc. *POINTS* value: *4.*

GOOD IDEA Instead of using sliced sweet onion, you can take the bite out of regular sliced onion by soaking the slices in ice water a few minutes.

¼ **cup** dried Italian seasoned bread crumbs

2 **tablespoons grated** Parmesan cheese

4 **(3-ounce) thin-sliced** chicken breast cutlets

1½ **teaspoons** olive oil

2 **cups** baby arugula

1 large tomato, **diced**

¼ **cup thinly sliced** Vidalia **or other sweet** onion

3 **tablespoons** light balsamic vinaigrette dressing

Freshly ground pepper, to taste

Cornmeal-Crusted Chicken with Peach Salsa

HANDS-ON PREP **5 MIN**
COOK **10 MIN**
SERVES **4**

1 Combine the peach, tomato, basil, vinegar, ¼ teaspoon of the salt, and ¼ teaspoon of pepper in a small bowl; set aside.

2 Mix the cornmeal and the remaining ½ teaspoon salt and ¼ teaspoon pepper on a sheet of wax paper. Press the chicken in the mixture to coat. Heat the oil in a large nonstick skillet over medium-high heat. Add the chicken and cook, turning occasionally, until lightly browned and cooked through, about 10 minutes. Serve the chicken with the salsa.

PER SERVING (1 piece chicken and generous ⅓ cup salsa): 238 Cal, 7 g Fat, 1 g Sat Fat, 0 g Trans Fat, 86 mg Chol, 524 mg Sod, 10 g Carb, 2 g Fib, 32 g Prot, 25 mg Calc. *POINTS* value: *5.*

GOOD IDEA If you can't find ripe peaches or nectarines for the salsa, ripe mango or papaya would be a delicious alternative.

1 large peach **or nectarine, pitted and finely chopped**

1 large tomato, **finely chopped**

¼ cup chopped fresh basil

2 teaspoons balsamic vinegar

¾ teaspoon salt

½ teaspoon freshly ground pepper

2 tablespoons yellow cornmeal

4 (5-ounce) skinless, boneless chicken breast halves

2 teaspoons canola oil

Cornmeal-Crusted Chicken
with Peach Salsa

Grilled Chicken with Persimmon
on Sweet Baby Greens

Grilled Chicken with Persimmon on Sweet Baby Greens

HANDS-ON PREP **12 MIN**
COOK **6 MIN**
SERVES **4**

1 Sprinkle the chicken with the oregano, ½ teaspoon of the salt, and the pepper.

2 Spray a nonstick ridged grill pan with nonstick spray and set over medium-high heat. Add the chicken and cook until browned on the outside and cooked through, about 3 minutes on each side. Transfer the chicken to a serving plate; cover lightly with foil to keep warm.

3 Meanwhile, combine the vinegar, onion, oil, preserves, and the remaining ⅛ teaspoon salt in a large bowl. Add the spinach and toss to coat. Arrange on a large platter.

4 Add the chicken to the spinach. Arrange the persimmon slices and the pomegranate seeds around the chicken and serve at once.

PER SERVING (1 cup spinach, 1 chicken cutlet, and 1 or 2 slices persimmon): 225 Cal, 7 g Fat, 2 g Sat Fat, 0 g Trans Fat, 68 mg Chol, 615 mg Sod, 14 g Carb, 4 g Fib, 27 g Prot, 73 mg Calc.
POINTS value: **4.**

TRY IT *Persimmon* (puhr-SIHM-muhn) are available from October through February. For best flavor, choose the small, tomato-shaped Fuyu persimmon. This persimmon is ripe and at its best when still firm. In fact, to get good slices, you don't want it to be too soft. If you can only find the larger Hachiya persimmon, you'll need to let it get fully ripe and soft before eating, otherwise it is too astringent.

4 (¼-pound) thin-sliced chicken breast cutlets

1 teaspoon dried oregano

¾ teaspoon salt

¼ teaspoon freshly ground pepper

2 tablespoons malt or cider vinegar

2 tablespoons finely chopped red onion

1 tablespoon extra-virgin olive oil

1 tablespoon all-fruit black cherry preserves

1 (7-ounce) package baby spinach trio (spinach, arugula, and shredded carrot)

1 Fuyu persimmon, peeled and thinly sliced

¼ cup pomegranate seeds

Red Thai Chicken Curry with Cauliflower

HANDS-ON PREP **5 MIN**
COOK **15 MIN**
SERVES **4**

1 Sprinkle the chicken with the salt. Heat ½ teaspoon of the oil in a large nonstick skillet over medium-high heat. Add the chicken and cook, turning occasionally, until browned and cooked through, about 5 minutes. Transfer the chicken to a plate.

2 Add the remaining ½ teaspoon oil to the same skillet, then add the bell pepper and scallions. Cook over medium-high heat, stirring often, until the scallions turn bright green, about 3 minutes. Add the curry paste and sugar; cook, stirring constantly, about 1 minute. Stir in the coconut milk, cauliflower, and carrots; bring to a boil. Reduce the heat and simmer, covered, stirring occasionally, until the vegetables are tender, about 6 minutes.

3 Return the chicken to the skillet and heat through, stirring occasionally, about 1 minute. Remove the skillet from the heat and stir in the basil.

PER SERVING (1½ cups): 276 Cal, 14 g Fat, 8 g Sat Fat, 0 g Trans Fat, 53 mg Chol, 331 mg Sod, 19 g Carb, 5 g Fib, 24 g Prot, 82 mg Calc. **POINTS** value: **6.**

GOOD IDEA Transform this easy curry from Thai to Indian by substituting Indian curry paste for the Thai red curry paste. Since the Indian variety is often not as hot as the Thai, you may need to add a little more of the Indian version.

¾ **pound** skinless, boneless chicken thighs, **cut into 1½-inch chunks**

¼ **teaspoon** salt

1 **teaspoon** canola oil

1 **yellow bell pepper, seeded and thinly sliced**

6 **scallions, cut into 1-inch pieces**

2½ **teaspoons** Thai red **curry paste**

2 **teaspoons** sugar

1 (14-ounce) **can** light (reduced-fat) coconut milk

1 (12-ounce) **bag** fresh **cauliflower florets**

1 (6-ounce) **bag** shredded carrots

½ **cup torn** fresh purple or green basil leaves

Yucatan Chicken and Tortilla Soup

HANDS-ON PREP **5 MIN**
COOK **15 MIN**
SERVES **4**

1 Bring the broth, onion, garlic, chili powder, and cumin to a boil in a large covered saucepan. Reduce the heat and simmer, covered, until the onion is almost tender, about 3 minutes.

2 Add the zucchini, black beans, tortilla chips, and the chipotle chile; return to a boil. Reduce the heat and simmer, covered, until the chips soften and the vegetables are tender, about 3 minutes.

3 Stir in the chicken and heat through, about 1 minute. Remove the saucepan from the heat, then stir in the cilantro and lime juice.

PER SERVING (1¾ cups): 282 Cal, 3 g Fat, 1 g Sat Fat, 0 g Trans Fat, 43 mg Chol, 1061 mg Sod, 40 g Carb, 7 g Fib, 28 g Prot, 108 mg Calc. **POINTS** value: **5.**

GOOD IDEA This dish is great made a day ahead but leave out the chips because they'll keep absorbing the liquid and the soup will become too thick. Instead, add them when reheating the soup, making sure to let it simmer a couple of minutes until the chips soften.

- **4 cups** reduced-sodium fat-free chicken broth
- **1 onion, chopped**
- **2 garlic cloves, minced**
- **1 teaspoon chili powder**
- **½ teaspoon** ground cumin
- **1 large zucchini, quartered lengthwise, then sliced**
- **1 (15½-ounce)** can black beans, **rinsed and drained**
- **1½ cups crumbled** low-fat baked tortilla chips
- **1** chipotle chile en adobo, **chopped**
- **1½ cups** shredded cooked chicken breast
- **½ cup chopped** fresh cilantro
- **2 tablespoons** fresh lime juice

Moroccan Chicken and Couscous Soup

HANDS-ON PREP **5 MIN**
COOK **10 MIN**
SERVES **6**

1 Bring the broth, chickpeas, tomatoes, carrots, cumin, turmeric, and cinnamon to a boil in a large covered saucepan. Reduce the heat and simmer, covered, until the carrots are tender, about 2 minutes. Add the chicken and heat through, about 1 minute.

2 Stir in the spinach and couscous. Remove from the heat, cover, and let stand until the couscous is tender and the spinach wilts, about 5 minutes.

PER SERVING (1½ cups): 274 Cal, 5 g Fat, 1 g Sat Fat, 0 g Trans Fat, 35 mg Chol, 849 mg Sod, 34 g Carb, 6 g Fib, 23 g Prot, 104 mg Calc. **POINTS** value: **5.**

TRY IT *Turmeric* (TER-muh-rihk) is the root of a plant similar to ginger. It has an intense yellow color and is used most frequently in curries, as an ingredient in yellow mustards, and as an inexpensive substitute for saffron.

4 **cups** reduced-sodium chicken broth

1 (15½-ounce) can chickpeas, **rinsed and drained**

1 (14½-ounce) can diced tomatoes with roasted garlic and onion

1 (6-ounce) bag shredded carrots

1 **teaspoon** ground cumin

¼ **teaspoon** turmeric

⅛ **teaspoon** cinnamon

1 (10-ounce) package sliced oven-roasted chicken breast, **cut into bite-size pieces**

1 (6-ounce) bag baby spinach

½ **cup** plain couscous

Moroccan Chicken and
Couscous Soup

Chicken Quesadillas with Creamy Salsa

HANDS-ON PREP **8 MIN**
COOK **6 MIN**
SERVES **4**

1 Preheat the oven to 450°F. Line a baking sheet with foil, then coat the foil with nonstick spray.

2 Meanwhile, place a tortilla on a work surface. Top half the tortilla with 2 tablespoons of the cheese, ¼ cup of the chicken, ¼ cup of the corn, scant ¼ cup of the roasted peppers, 1 tablespoon of the cilantro, then 2 tablespoons more cheese. Fold the top half of the tortilla over the filling to form a semicircle, lightly pressing the edges to seal. Repeat with the remaining ingredients making 4 quesadillas.

3 Place the quesadillas on the baking sheet; lightly spray the quesadillas with nonstick spray. Bake until lightly browned, about 6 minutes.

4 Meanwhile, combine the sour cream, salsa, and the remaining ¼ cup cilantro in a small bowl. Serve with the quesadillas.

PER SERVING (1 quesadilla and 2 tablespoons salsa): 360 Cal, 9 g Fat, 4 g Sat Fat, 0 g Trans Fat, 49 mg Chol, 998 mg Sod, 46 g Carb, 3 g Fib, 24 g Prot, 285 mg Calc. *POINTS* value: *7.*

4 (8-inch) fat-free flour tortillas

1 cup shredded reduced-fat Mexican cheese blend

1 cup shredded cooked chicken breast

1 (8¾-ounce) can corn, drained

1 (7-ounce) jar roasted peppers, drained and cut in half

½ cup chopped fresh cilantro

¼ cup fat-free sour cream

¼ cup salsa, preferably refrigerated fresh

Warm Chicken, Apple, and Curried Couscous Salad

HANDS-ON PREP **5 MIN**
COOK **5 MIN**
SERVES **6**

1 Bring the water, 1 teaspoon of the curry powder, and ½ teaspoon of the salt to a boil in a small saucepan. Add the couscous; cover and remove from the heat. Let stand 5 minutes, then fluff with a fork.

2 Combine the chickpeas, apple, chicken, scallions, lemon juice, olive oil, and the remaining ¼ teaspoon curry powder and ¼ teaspoon salt in a large bowl. Add the couscous and mix well. Divide the spinach among 6 plates. Spoon the couscous salad evenly (about 1 cup) on each plate.

PER SERVING (1 salad): 267 Cal, 4 g Fat, 1 g Sat Fat, 0 g Trans Fat, 19 mg Chol, 411 mg Sod, 42 g Carb, 6 g Fib, 16 g Prot, 72 mg Calc. **POINTS** value: **5.**

GOOD IDEA For extra crunch, sprinkle 1 tablespoon coarsely chopped unsalted roasted almonds on each serving (remember to deduct them from your **weekly POINTS Allowance**—1 tablespoon will increase the **POINTS** value by 1). No need to heat up the oven to toast the nuts. Jarred or packaged unsalted roasted almonds are a great time-saver. Store the leftover nuts in the freezer to keep them fresh.

1½ **cups** water

1¼ **teaspoons curry powder**

¾ **teaspoon salt**

1 **cup plain couscous**

1 **(15½-ounce) can chickpeas (garbanzo beans), rinsed and drained**

1 **red apple, unpeeled and diced**

1 **cup diced cooked chicken breast**

2 **scallions, sliced**

3 **tablespoons fresh lemon juice**

2 **teaspoons extra-virgin olive oil**

1 **(6-ounce) bag baby spinach**

Tuscan Chicken
Sausage Stew

Tuscan Chicken Sausage Stew

HANDS-ON PREP **5 MIN**
COOK **10 MIN**
SERVES **4**

1 Spray a large nonstick skillet with nonstick spray; set over high heat. Add the sausages, mushrooms, and zucchini; cook, stirring frequently, until the sausages and vegetables are lightly browned, about 6 minutes.

2 Stir in the beans, diced tomatoes, tomato sauce, water, and rosemary; bring to a boil. Reduce the heat and simmer, uncovered, until the vegetables are tender, about 2 minutes. Remove from the heat and stir in the arugula until it wilts, about 1 minute.

PER SERVING (1½ cups): 249 Cal, 6 g Fat, 2 g Sat Fat, 0 g Trans Fat, 24 mg Chol, 1079 mg Sod, 34 g Carb, 8 g Fib, 18 g Prot, 89 mg Calc. **POINTS** value: **5.**

EXPRESS LANE If you want to plan ahead for an instant meal later in the week, this stew can be refrigerated up to 2 days, which will give the flavors a chance to develop. (But it's preferable to stir in the arugula just before serving.) Low-fat, multi-grain crackers make a good, crunchy accompaniment.

6 ounces fully cooked Italian-style chicken sausages (preferably artichoke and garlic), diced

1 (10-ounce) package sliced mushrooms

1 medium zucchini, diced

1 (15½-ounce) can cannellini (white kidney) beans, rinsed and drained

1 (14½-ounce) can diced tomatoes with roasted garlic and onion

1 (8-ounce) can tomato sauce

¼ cup water

2 teaspoons chopped fresh rosemary

2 cups baby arugula

Chicken Sausages Provençal on Polenta

HANDS-ON PREP **5 MIN**
COOK **15 MIN**
SERVES **4**

1 Preheat the oven to 450°F. Line a baking sheet with foil, then spray the foil with nonstick spray. Arrange the polenta slices in a single layer on the foil. Spray lightly with nonstick spray and bake until golden, about 9 minutes.

2 Meanwhile, spray a large nonstick skillet with nonstick spray and set over medium-high heat. Add the bell pepper and onion; cook, stirring often, until softened, about 3 minutes. Stir in the sausage and fennel seeds; cook until the sausage is lightly browned, about 2 minutes.

3 Stir the sauce, water, and olives into the skillet; bring to a boil over medium-high heat. Reduce the heat and simmer, stirring occasionally, until the vegetables are tender, about 1 minute. Remove from the heat and stir in the basil.

4 Transfer the polenta to a serving platter and top with sausage mixture.

PER SERVING (3 slices polenta and ¾ cup sausage mixture): 238 Cal, 9 g Fat, 2 g Sat Fat, 0 g Trans Fat, 33 mg Chol, 900 mg Sod, 28 g Carb, 3 g Fib, 13 g Prot, 49 mg Calc. **POINTS** value: **5.**

FOOD NOTE Fully cooked chicken sausages are a great time-saver because they only need a few minutes of heating through. They vary in fat content—look for ones that have 10 grams or less of fat per serving.

1 (16-ounce) tube fat-free polenta, cut into 12 (½-inch) slices

1 large yellow bell pepper, seeded and sliced

1 large onion, sliced

½ pound fully cooked sun-dried tomato chicken sausages, cut into 1-inch-thick chunks

½ teaspoon fennel seeds

1 cup jarred fat-free marinara sauce

⅓ cup water

6 kalamata olives, pitted and chopped

½ cup chopped fresh basil

Thai Coconut-Chicken Soup

HANDS-ON PREP **5 MIN**
COOK **12 MIN**
SERVES **4**

1 Trim away the tops of the lemongrass, about 4 inches from the root end; trim away the root. Crush the 4-inch pieces with the side of a knife and mince the tender white inner stalk; discard the outer stalk.

2 Heat the oil in a nonstick Dutch oven over medium-high heat. Add the minced lemongrass, garlic, and crushed red pepper; cook, stirring constantly, until fragrant, about 45 seconds. Add the chicken and cook, breaking it apart with a wooden spoon, until browned, about 3 minutes.

3 Add the chicken broth, coconut milk, lime juice, and fish sauce; bring to a boil. Add the rice sticks and cook until translucent, about 3 minutes. Remove from the heat and stir in the cilantro.

PER SERVING (1½ cups): 276 Cal, 10 g Fat, 6 g Sat Fat, 0 g Trans Fat, 34 mg Chol, 756 mg Sod, 30 g Carb, 1 g Fib, 19 g Prot, 34 mg Calc. **POINTS** value: **6.**

FOOD NOTE Coconut milk is made from coconut flesh steeped in water, then pressed out as milk. Light or reduced-fat coconut milk is simply the second pressing of the same coconut solids, with far less fat in the milk. Look for coconut milk in the ethnic food section of the supermarket.

2 stalks fresh lemongrass, **minced**

2 teaspoons olive oil

1 garlic clove, **minced**

½ teaspoon crushed red pepper

½ pound ground skinless chicken breast

2 (14½-ounce) cans reduced-sodium chicken broth

1 (14-ounce) can light (reduced-fat) coconut milk

1 tablespoon fresh lime juice

1**½** teaspoons Asian fish sauce (nam pla)

4 ounces rice sticks (mai fun)

3 tablespoons chopped fresh cilantro

Mexican Sloppy Joe Tortilla Cups

HANDS-ON PREP **5 MIN**
COOK **10 MIN**
SERVES **4**

1 Preheat the oven to 400°F. Place 4 (10-ounce) custard cups on a baking sheet. Spray the insides of the cups with nonstick spray. Gently press a tortilla into each cup. Bake until golden and crisp, about 8 minutes. Let the tortillas cool in the cups, about 2 minutes. Carefully transfer the tortilla cups to a plate.

2 Meanwhile, heat the oil in a large nonstick skillet over medium-high heat. Add the chicken, salt, and pepper; cook, breaking the chicken apart with a wooden spoon, until browned, about 6 minutes. Stir in the salsa and heat through, about 3 minutes.

3 Mix the mayonnaise, onion, lime zest, and lime juice in a small bowl. Spoon about ¾ cup chicken mixture into each tortilla cup and top each with 1½ tablespoons of the mayonnaise mixture.

PER SERVING (1 filled tortilla cup): 337 Cal, 7 g Fat, 2 g Sat Fat, 0 g Trans Fat, 70 mg Chol, 816 mg Sod, 36 g Carb, 5 g Fib, 31 g Prot, 61 mg Calc. **POINTS** value: **7.**

EXPRESS LANE Double the chicken filling and freeze half for up to 3 months and serve with tortillas for another tasty meal in a flash.

4 (6-inch) fat-free flour tortillas

2 teaspoons olive oil

1 pound ground skinless chicken breast

¼ teaspoon salt

¼ teaspoon freshly ground pepper

1½ cups jarred black bean and corn salsa

¼ cup fat-free mayonnaise

¼ cup finely chopped, red onion

2 teaspoons grated lime zest

1 tablespoon lime juice

Mexican Sloppy Joe
Tortilla Cups

French Chicken Burger

HANDS-ON PREP **5 MIN**
COOK **10 MIN**
SERVES **4**

1 Spray the broiler rack with nonstick spray; preheat the broiler. Combine the chicken, bread crumbs, mustard, shallot, tarragon, herbes de Provence, salt, and pepper in a medium bowl. Form into 4 oval-shaped burgers, about ½ inch thick.

2 Place the burgers on the broiler rack and broil 4 inches from the heat until an instant-read thermometer inserted in the side of each burger registers 165°F, 5–6 minutes on each side.

3 Meanwhile, brush the bread with the oil and broil, alongside the burgers, until lightly toasted, about 3 minutes. Rub the cut-sides of the garlic over the toasted bread. Top each piece of garlic toast with a burger.

PER SERVING (1 burger): 408 Cal, 9 g Fat, 2 g Sat Fat, 1 g Trans Fat, 68 mg Chol, 1054 mg Sod, 45 g Carb, 3 g Fib, 33 g Prot, 101 mg Calc. **POINTS** value: **8.**

TRY IT *Herbes de Provence* (EHRB duh proh-VAWNS) is a mixture of light herbs popular in southern French cooking. It often contains lavender, thyme, chervil, and savory.

- 1 **pound** ground skinless chicken breast
- 2 **tablespoons** dried plain bread crumbs
- 2 **tablespoons** Dijon mustard
- 1 **shallot,** minced
- 1 **teaspoon** dried tarragon
- ½ **teaspoon** herbes de Provence
- ½ **teaspoon** salt
- ¼ **teaspoon** freshly ground pepper
- 2 **(4½-inch-long) pieces** French bread, **halved horizontally**
- 2 **teaspoons** olive oil
- 1 **garlic clove, halved lengthwise**

Pasta Bolognese with Mushrooms

HANDS-ON PREP **5 MIN**
COOK **15 MIN**
SERVES **4**

1 Bring 3 quarts of water to a boil in a large saucepan; set over high heat.

2 Meanwhile, heat the oil in a large nonstick skillet over medium-high heat. Add the onion and garlic; cook, stirring frequently, until light golden brown, about 4 minutes. Add the chicken and cook, breaking it apart with a wooden spoon until browned, about 3 minutes. Add the mushrooms, salt, and pepper; cook, stirring occasionally, about 2 minutes. Add the tomato sauce and vinegar; bring to a simmer.

3 Meanwhile, add the pasta to the boiling water and cook until al dente, about 2 minutes. Drain, reserving ½ cup of the pasta cooking water. Mix the pasta with the mushroom mixture, adding the reserved water to moisten.

PER SERVING (1½ cups): 329 Cal, 8 g Fat, 2 g Sat Fat, 0 g Trans Fat, 75 mg Chol, 682 mg Sod, 42 g Carb, 4 g Fib, 22 g Prot, 45 mg Calc. **POINTS** value: **6.**

GOOD IDEA Depending on the season, look for baby bella, shiitake, cremini, porcini, or morel mushrooms— they often come in packages already sliced.

4 **teaspoons** olive oil

1 **onion, finely chopped**

3 **garlic cloves, sliced**

½ **pound** ground skinless chicken breast

1 **(12-ounce) package** sliced fresh mushrooms

½ **teaspoon** salt

½ **teaspoon** freshly ground pepper

1 **(8-ounce)** can tomato sauce

2 **tablespoons** balsamic vinegar

1 **(9-ounce) package** fresh fettuccine

Chicken and Bean Picadillo

HANDS-ON PREP **5 MIN**
COOK **10 MIN**
SERVES **4**

1 Heat the oil in a large nonstick skillet over medium-high heat. Add the onion and garlic; cook, stirring frequently, until light golden brown, about 3 minutes. Add the chicken and cook, breaking it apart with a wooden spoon, until browned, about 2 minutes. Add the salt, cinnamon, cumin, and pepper; cook, stirring occasionally, about 30 seconds.

2 Add the beans and tomatoes; bring to a boil. Reduce the heat and simmer, uncovered, stirring occasionally, until slightly thickened, about 3 minutes.

PER SERVING (1 cup): 219 Cal, 5 g Fat, 1 g Sat Fat, 0 g Trans Fat, 34 mg Chol, 658 mg Sod, 25 g Carb, 6 g Fib, 20 g Prot, 73 mg Calc. *POINTS* value: **4.**

GOOD IDEA Raisins would make a sweet addition to this dish—add ½ cup with the beans and tomatoes, but remember to deduct them from your **weekly** *POINTS* **Allowance** (½ cup raisins for 4 servings will increase the per-serving *POINTS* value by 1).

2 teaspoons olive oil

1 onion, finely chopped

3 garlic cloves, minced

½ pound ground skinless chicken breast

½ teaspoon salt

½ teaspoon cinnamon

¼ teaspoon ground cumin

¼ teaspoon freshly ground pepper

1 (15½-ounce) can cannellini (white kidney) beans, rinsed and drained

1 (14½-ounce) can fire-roasted diced tomatoes

Turkey Cutlets with Cranberry-Nut Topping

HANDS-ON PREP **5 MIN**
COOK **10 MIN**
SERVES **4**

1 Preheat the broiler. Place an oven rack 4 inches from the heat source.

2 Sprinkle the turkey with the salt and pepper. Heat the oil in a large ovenproof skillet over medium-high heat. Add the turkey cutlets and cook until browned and cooked through, about 3 minutes on each side. Remove skillet from the heat.

3 Meanwhile, combine the nuts, cranberries, bread crumbs, and orange zest in a small bowl. Sprinkle the mixture evenly over each turkey cutlet, then top each with ½ tablespoon cheese. Place the skillet on the oven rack and broil 4 inches from the heat until the cheese is lightly browned, 1–2 minutes.

PER SERVING (1 cutlet): 219 Cal, 8 g Fat, 2 g Sat Fat, 0 g Trans Fat, 79 mg Chol, 394 mg Sod, 7 g Carb, 1 g Fib, 28 g Prot, 46 mg Calc. *POINTS* value: **5.**

HOW WE DID IT You'll need an ovenproof skillet for this recipe: While cast iron is good, skillets with nonstick coatings are not suitable for placing under the high heat of a broiler. If your skillet has a non ovenproof handle, simply wrap the handle with a double layer of foil.

4 (¼-pound) **turkey breast cutlets**

½ **teaspoon salt**

¼ **teaspoon freshly ground pepper**

1 **teaspoon olive oil**

¼ **cup chopped pecans or walnuts**

2 **tablespoons chopped dried cranberries**

2 **tablespoons dried plain bread crumbs**

1 **teaspoon grated orange zest**

2 **tablespoons shredded manchego or sharp cheddar cheese**

**Parmesan-Crusted Turkey
with Tomato-Lemon Sauté**

Parmesan-Crusted Turkey with Tomato-Lemon Sauté

HANDS-ON PREP **10 MIN**
COOK **10 MIN**
SERVES **4**

1 Combine the tomatoes, lemon zest, and ¼ teaspoon of the salt in a medium bowl; set aside.

2 Whisk the egg white and lemon juice on a large shallow plate. Combine the cornmeal, Parmesan cheese, pepper, and remaining ¼ teaspoon salt on a sheet of wax paper.

3 Dip each cutlet into the egg mixture, then coat in the cornmeal mixture.

4 Heat the oil in a large nonstick skillet over medium-high heat. Add the cutlets and cook until browned and cooked through, about 3 minutes on each side. Transfer the cutlets to a serving plate.

5 Add the tomato mixture to the same skillet and cook, stirring frequently, until heated through, about 1 minute. Serve with the cutlets.

PER SERVING (1 cutlet and ¼ cup tomatoes): 224 Cal, 7 g Fat, 2 g Sat Fat, 0 g Trans Fat, 77 mg Chol, 423 mg Sod, 10 g Carb, 2 g Fib, 30 g Prot, 63 mg Calc. **POINTS** value: **5.**

GOOD IDEA For the tastiest cheese crust, seek out authentic Parmigiano-Reggiano cheese and grate or shred it yourself.

1 **pint** grape **or** cherry tomatoes, **halved**

2 **teaspoons grated** lemon zest

½ **teaspoon** salt

1 **egg white**

1 **tablespoon** fresh lemon juice

3 **tablespoons** cornmeal

2 **tablespoons grated** Parmesan cheese

¼ **teaspoon** freshly ground pepper

4 **(¼-pound)** turkey breast cutlets

4 **teaspoons** olive oil

Chinese Meatballs with Bok Choy

HANDS-ON PREP **5 MIN**
COOK **15 MIN**
SERVES **4**

1 Combine the turkey, 2 tablespoons of the teriyaki sauce, the scallions, ginger, and garlic in a bowl. Form into 12 meatballs.

2 Heat the oil in a large nonstick skillet over medium-high heat. Add the meatballs and cook, partially covered, until cooked through and browned, turning occasionally, about 12 minutes. Transfer the meatballs to a plate and keep warm.

3 Add the hoisin sauce, 2 tablespoons water, and remaining 1 tablespoon teriyaki sauce to the skillet, scraping up any browned bits from the bottom of the skillet. Cook until slightly thickened, about 1 minute.

4 Meanwhile, place the bok choy in a saucepan with 2 tablespoons water, cover, and cook until fork-tender, about 5 minutes. Drain and transfer to a serving bowl; toss with the sesame oil. Place the meatballs on top and drizzle with the sauce.

PER SERVING (3 meatballs, ½ cup bok choy, and 1½ tablespoons sauce): 222 Cal, 6 g Fat, 1 g Sat Fat, 0 g Trans Fat, 75 mg Chol, 901 mg Sod, 13 g Carb, 2 g Fib, 30 g Prot, 159 mg Calc.
POINTS value: **5.**

HOW WE DID IT When shaping meatballs, moisten your hands with a little water if the mixture begins to stick to your hands.

1 **pound** ground skinless turkey breast

3 **tablespoons** teriyaki sauce

3 scallions, **finely** chopped

2 **teaspoons grated peeled** fresh ginger

2 garlic cloves, **minced**

2 **teaspoons** canola oil

¼ **cup** hoisin sauce

1 **pound** bok choy, **coarsely chopped, about 4 cups**

1 **teaspoon** Asian (dark) sesame oil

Turkish Turkey Burger

HANDS-ON PREP **5 MIN**
COOK **15 MIN**
SERVES **4**

1 Spray the broiler rack with nonstick spray; preheat the broiler.

2 Place the pine nuts in a medium nonstick skillet over medium heat and cook, stirring frequently, until golden brown, about 4 minutes. Add the cumin and cinnamon and cook until fragrant, about 1 minute. Transfer to a large mixing bowl.

3 Heat the oil in the same skillet over medium-high heat. Add the onion and cook, stirring constantly, until translucent, about 2 minutes. Add to the nuts in the bowl. Add the turkey, egg white, salt, and pepper and mix well. Form into 4 burgers.

4 Arrange the burgers on the broiler rack; broil 4 inches from the heat until an instant-read thermometer inserted in the side of a burger registers 165°F, 5–6 minutes on each side. Serve the burgers in the pitas with a slice of tomato.

PER SERVING (1 burger): 356 Cal, 9 g Fat, 2 g Sat Fat, 0 g Trans Fat, 75 mg Chol, 653 mg Sod, 35 g Carb, 6 g Fib, 35 g Prot, 36 mg Calc. **POINTS** value: **7.**

GOOD IDEA While this dish is flavorful enough to stand on its own, a small scoop of baba ghanouj complements it nicely (1 generous tablespoon will increase the **POINTS** value by 1).

¼ cup **pine nuts**

½ **teaspoon** ground cumin

½ **teaspoon** cinnamon

2 **teaspoons** olive oil

½ **small yellow onion,** grated

1 **pound** ground skinless turkey breast

1 **egg white**

½ **teaspoon** salt

¼ **teaspoon** freshly ground pepper

4 **(6-inch)** whole-wheat pita breads

1 **large tomato, cut into 4 thick slices**

Curried Turkey Burger with Rice

HANDS-ON PREP **5 MIN**
COOK **10 MIN**
SERVES **4**

1 Spray the broiler rack with nonstick spray; preheat the broiler.

2 Combine the turkey, ¼ cup of the yogurt, the onion, bread crumbs, curry powder, salt, and pepper in a medium bowl. Form into 4 burgers.

3 Arrange the burgers on the broiler rack; broil 4 inches from the heat until an instant-read thermometer inserted in the side of a burger registers 165°F, 5–6 minutes on each side.

4 Meanwhile, cook the rice according to package directions, omitting the salt, if desired. Serve the burgers on the rice with the remaining ¼ cup yogurt and the chutney.

PER SERVING (1 burger, ⅔ cup rice, 1 tablespoon yogurt, and 2 tablespoons chutney): 380 Cal, 3 g Fat, 1 g Sat Fat, 0 g Trans Fat, 77 mg Chol, 409 mg Sod, 53 g Carb, 7 g Fib, 33 g Prot, 101 mg Calc. **POINTS** value: **7.**

FOOD NOTE Curry powder—a mix of spices, herbs, and seeds, such as coriander, fenugreek, cumin, fennel, cinnamon, and cloves—can vary dramatically in flavor and heat intensity. If you like hot curry flavor, choose Madras curry powder, which is a hotter variety of curry powder.

1 **pound** ground skinless turkey breast

½ **cup** plain low-fat yogurt

½ **small onion, grated**

1 **tablespoon** dried plain bread crumbs

1 **tablespoon** curry powder

½ **teaspoon** salt

¼ **teaspoon** freshly ground pepper

2 **cups** quick-cooking brown rice

½ **cup** bottled mango chutney

Tomato-Basil Soup with Turkey

HANDS-ON PREP **5 MIN**
COOK **15 MIN**
SERVES **4**

1 Heat the oil in a Dutch oven over medium-high heat. Add the onion and carrot; cook, stirring occasionally, until softened, about 5 minutes. Add the broth, tomatoes, sugar, salt, and pepper; bring to a boil. Reduce the heat and simmer, about 5 minutes.

2 Puree the mixture with an immersible blender. Add the turkey and half-and-half and heat through, about 3 minutes. Stir in basil.

PER SERVING (2 cups): 196 Cal, 4 g Fat, 1 g Sat Fat, 0 g Trans Fat, 39 mg Chol, 864 mg Sod, 21 g Carb, 3 g Fib, 20 g Prot, 128 mg Calc. *POINTS* value: *4.*

FOOD NOTE **If you don't have an immersible hand held blender, puree the soup, in batches, in a regular blender.**

2 **teaspoons** olive oil

1 **large onion, finely chopped**

1 **carrot, shredded**

2 **(14½-ounce) cans reduced-sodium chicken broth**

1 **(28-ounce) can fire-roasted crushed tomatoes**

½ **teaspoon** sugar

½ **teaspoon** salt

¼ **teaspoon** freshly ground pepper

6 **ounces cooked turkey breast, cubed**

½ **cup fat-free half-and-half**

¼ **cup thinly sliced fresh basil leaves**

Pasta with Sausage, Spinach, and Pine Nuts

HANDS-ON PREP **5 MIN**
COOK **15 MIN**
SERVES **4**

1 Bring 3 quarts of water to a boil in a large saucepan, over high heat.

2 Meanwhile heat the oil in a large nonstick skillet over medium-high heat. Add the sausage and cook until lightly browned, about 4 minutes. Add the pine nuts, garlic, and crushed red pepper; cook, stirring frequently until the nuts are lightly browned and the sausage is dark brown, about 2 minutes.

3 Add the pasta to the boiling water and cook until al dente, about 2 minutes. Drain, reserving ½ cup of the pasta cooking water. Return the pasta to the saucepan; add the sausage mixture, spinach, and the reserved water; toss to coat.

PER SERVING (1½ cups): 333 Cal, 13 g Fat, 3 g Sat Fat, 0 g Trans Fat, 74 mg Chol, 418 mg Sod, 36 g Carb, 4 g Fib, 18 g Prot, 89 mg Calc. **POINTS** value: **7.**

FOOD NOTE Reserving some of the pasta's starchy cooking water is a good idea. Cooked pasta tends to soak up a lot of whatever sauce is coating it and the reserved water can add moistness.

2 **teaspoons** olive oil

½ **pound** hot Italian turkey sausage, **cut into ¼-inch-thick rounds**

2 **tablespoons** pine nuts

1 **garlic clove,** minced

¼ **teaspoon** crushed red pepper

1 **(9-ounce) package** fresh fettuccine

1 **(9-ounce) bag baby spinach**

Pasta with Sausage, Spinach, and Pine Nuts

Turkey Salad with Orange and Fennel

HANDS-ON PREP **20 MIN**
COOK **NONE**
SERVES **4**

1 Grate 2 teaspoons of zest from the oranges; set aside. Cut the peel and pith from the oranges; slice the oranges into 12 rounds; set aside.

2 Whisk the olive oil, vinegar, fennel, mustard, salt, pepper, and orange zest in a small bowl.

3 Toss together the lettuce and fennel in a salad bowl. Top with the turkey, tomato, and onion. Arrange the orange slices around the outside rim of the bowl. Drizzle the salad with the dressing. Toss just before serving.

PER SERVING (about 3 cups): 207 Cal, 7 g Fat, 1 g Sat Fat, 0 g Trans Fat, 49 mg Chol, 558 mg Sod, 18 g Carb, 6 g Fib, 20 g Prot, 106 mg Calc. **POINTS** value: **4.**

GOOD IDEA This dressing can be doubled and kept in the refrigerator for up to 5 days. Extra dressing is delicious on a baby spinach salad.

2 navel oranges

5 teaspoons olive oil

4 teaspoons cider vinegar

½ teaspoon ground fennel seeds

½ teaspoon mustard powder

½ teaspoon salt

¼ teaspoon freshly ground pepper

1 small head romaine lettuce, coarsely chopped

1 fennel bulb, cored and cut into ¼-inch-thick strips

½ pound cooked turkey breast, cut into ¼-inch-thick strips

1 beefsteak tomato, coarsely chopped

½ small red onion, finely chopped

Duck Tostadas

HANDS-ON PREP **5 MIN**
COOK **15 MIN**
SERVES **4**

1 Make about 4 diagonal slashes ¼ inch deep in skin of duck breast. Sprinkle the duck with the salt and pepper. Place a large nonstick skillet over medium-high heat. Add the duck and cook until cooked through, 4-5 minutes on each side. Place the duck on paper towels and let stand about 5 minutes. Remove the skin, then thinly slice the duck across the grain.

2 Meanwhile, cook the tortillas, one at a time, in a medium nonstick skillet, over high heat until crisped, about 40 seconds on each side. On each tortilla, spread 1 teaspoon mustard and sprinkle 2 tablespoons cheese. Evenly arrange the duck slices and apple wedges alternately in a circular pattern over the tortillas; sprinkle with the cilantro.

PER SERVING (1 tostada): 245 Cal, 4 g Fat, 2 g Sat Fat, 0 g Trans Fat, 64 mg Chol, 819 mg Sod, 24 g Carb, 2 g Fib, 28 g Prot, 168 mg Calc. **POINTS** value: **5.**

FOOD NOTE Duck breast can be found in gourmet grocery stores, fresh from late spring to early winter or frozen year-round. Muscovy duck breast halves range in weight from 8 ounces to 1 pound each. You can substitute boneless chicken thighs if you like.

- 1 **pound boneless duck breast (skin on)**
- ½ **teaspoon salt**
- ¼ **teaspoon freshly ground pepper**
- 4 **(6-inch) fat-free flour tortillas**
- 4 **teaspoons Dijon mustard**
- ½ **cup shredded reduced-fat Mexican cheese blend**
- 1 **apple, cored and sliced into thin wedges**
- 1 **tablespoon chopped fresh cilantro**

Fresh Fish Dishes

p 119

p 138

p 144

CHAPTER 5

Asian Salmon Strips with
Watercress and Scallions

Asian Salmon Strips with Watercress and Scallions

HANDS-ON PREP **15 MIN**
COOK **5 MIN**
SERVES **4**

1 Combine the vinegar, ginger, soy sauce, honey, garlic, and 1 teaspoon of the oil in a large bowl; transfer 2 tablespoons of the mixture to a medium bowl. Add the salmon to the mixture in the medium bowl; toss to coat.

2 Heat the remaining 1 teaspoon oil in a large nonstick skillet over medium-high heat. Add the salmon and cook until lightly browned on the outside and opaque in the center, about 2 minutes on each side.

3 Add the watercress to the remaining vinegar mixture in the large bowl; toss to coat. Arrange the watercress on 4 plates. Top each with 2 of the salmon strips, then sprinkle with the scallions and sesame seeds.

PER SERVING (1 cup salad and 2 salmon strips): 220 Cal, 10 g Fat, 2 g Sat Fat, 0 g Trans Fat, 74 mg Chol, 225 mg Sod, 7 g Carb, 1 g Fib, 26 g Prot, 104 mg Calc. **POINTS** value: **5.**

GOOD IDEA Serve this dish with small seaweed or sesame rice crackers (6 or 7 will increase the **POINTS** value by 1).

2 tablespoons rice-wine vinegar

1 tablespoon grated peeled fresh ginger

1 tablespoon reduced-sodium soy sauce

1 tablespoon honey

1 garlic clove, minced

2 teaspoons Asian (dark) sesame oil

1 pound skinless salmon fillet, cut crosswise into 8 strips

2 (4-ounce) packages watercress or arugula

2 scallions (white and light green portion only), sliced

1 tablespoon sesame seeds

Microwave-Poached Salmon with Lemon-Dill Sauce

HANDS-ON PREP **10 MIN**

COOK **5 MIN**

SERVES **4**

1 Spray a 2-quart microwavable dish with a lid with nonstick spray. Add the salmon and sprinkle with the lemon juice, salt, and pepper. Cover the dish with the lid and microwave on High until the fish is just opaque in the center, 5-6 minutes, then let stand with the lid on for 1 minute. Drain the liquid from the fish into a cup. Cover the fish to keep it warm.

2 Meanwhile, mix the flour with about ¼ cup of the milk to a smooth paste in a medium saucepan. Stir in the remaining milk, the dill, lemon zest, and coriander. Cook, stirring constantly, until the mixture bubbles and thickens about 3 minutes. Stir in the fish liquid and reheat. Serve the salmon with the sauce.

PER SERVING (1 piece salmon with generous ¼ cup sauce): 245 Cal, 9 g Fat, 3 g Sat Fat, 0 g Trans Fat, 96 mg Chol, 560 mg Sod, 7 g Carb, 0 g Fib, 33 g Prot, 98 mg Calc. **POINTS** value: **6.**

ZAP IT For a quick accompaniment, check your supermarket ethnic food section for a pouch of precooked (cook-in-a-bag) basmati rice, which is ready to eat after microwaving for just 90 seconds (½ cup cooked rice will up the **POINTS** value by 2).

1¼ **pounds** skinless salmon fillet, **cut into 4 pieces**

2 **tablespoons** fresh lemon juice

¾ **teaspoon** salt

⅛ **teaspoon** ground white pepper

2 **tablespoons** all-purpose flour

1 **cup** low-fat (1%) milk

¼ **cup** chopped fresh dill

1 **teaspoon** grated lemon zest

¼ **teaspoon** ground coriander

Pan-Seared Salmon with Balsamic Drizzle

HANDS-ON PREP **10 MIN**
COOK **10 MIN**
SERVES **4**

1 To make the drizzle, bring the vinegar and sugar to a boil in a medium saucepan; boil rapidly until it is reduced to about ¼ cup, about 4 minutes. Remove from the heat and let cool 2 minutes. Combine the onion, oil, and ¼ teaspoon of the salt in a small jug; add the vinegar and set aside.

2 Sprinkle the salmon with the remaining ¼ teaspoon salt and the pepper. Spray a nonstick skillet or a nonstick ridged grill pan with nonstick spray and set over medium-high heat. Add the salmon and cook until just opaque in the center, about 3 minutes on each side.

3 Divide the mesclun among 4 plates; top each with a piece of salmon and sprinkle with the drizzle.

PER SERVING (1 piece salmon, 1 cup mesclun, and scant 2 tablespoons drizzle): 220 Cal, 10 g Fat, 2 g Sat Fat, 0 g Trans Fat, 74 mg Chol, 398 mg Sod, 7 g Carb, 2 g Fib, 25 g Prot, 61 mg Calc. **POINTS** value: **5.**

HOW WE DID IT You can cook the salmon with or without the skin. While removing it allows you to brown both sides of the fish, leaving it on helps hold the shape of the piece of salmon. If you do leave the skin on, avoid eating it because of its extra fat and calories.

½ cup **balsamic vinegar**

1 tablespoon packed **brown sugar**

2 tablespoons finely chopped **red onion**

1 tablespoon **extra-virgin olive oil**

½ teaspoon **salt**

4 (¼-pound) pieces **salmon fillet** (about 1 inch thick)

½ teaspoon **coarsely ground black pepper**

1 (6-ounce) **bag mesclun salad greens** (about 4 cups)

Tuna, Roasted Pepper, and Tzatziki Sandwiches

HANDS-ON PREP **15 MIN**
COOK **5 MIN**
SERVES **4**

1 Sprinkle both sides of the tuna with the salt and pepper. Heat the oil in a large nonstick skillet over medium-high heat. Add the tuna and cook until browned on the outside but still pink in the center, 2–3 minutes on each side for medium-rare.

2 Meanwhile, evenly spread the tzatziki on one side of each of the toasted bread slices. Place 5 basil leaves on each of 4 slices of bread; top each with one-fourth of the onion slices, one-fourth of the roasted red peppers, and a tuna steak. Place the remaining 4 bread slices on top of the tuna. Cut each sandwich in half with a serrated knife and serve at once.

PER SERVING (1 sandwich): 414 Cal, 13 g Fat, 4 g Sat Fat, 0 g Trans Fat, 88 mg Chol, 798 mg Sod, 38 g Carb, 6 g Fib, 38 g Prot, 214 mg Calc. **POINTS** value: **9.**

GOOD IDEA You can buy freshly baked whole-wheat and whole-grain boules (basically, round loaves of bread) in many supermarkets and bakeries. Have someone slice it for you and keep it in the freezer, taking out a few slices, as you need them.

4 (5-ounce) tuna steaks

½ teaspoon salt

¼ teaspoon freshly ground pepper

1 teaspoon extra-virgin olive oil

1 (7-ounce, 1-cup) container refrigerated tzatziki sauce

8 slices whole-grain or whole-wheat bread, about 3 x 5 inches, toasted

20 fresh basil leaves

1 small red onion, thinly sliced

1 (7½-ounce) jar roasted red peppers, drained

Tuna, Roasted Pepper, and
Tzatziki Sandwiches

Tex-Mex Tilapia, Tomato, and Corn Stew

HANDS-ON PREP **5 MIN**
COOK **15 MIN**
SERVES **4**

1 Heat the oil in a nonstick Dutch oven over medium-high heat. Add the onion and garlic; cook, stirring frequently, until light golden, about 3 minutes. Add the bell pepper and cook, stirring frequently, until softened, about 2 minutes.

2 Add the tomatoes, corn, salt, and cinnamon; bring to a boil, stirring occasionally. Add the tilapia, stirring gently to coat the fish with the sauce; return to a boil. Reduce the heat and simmer, covered, until the fish is just opaque in the center, about 6 minutes. Serve the stew in bowls; sprinkle with the cilantro and serve with the lime wedges.

PER SERVING (about 1⅓ cups): 221 Cal, 4 g Fat, 1 g Sat Fat, 0 g Trans Fat, 60 mg Chol, 398 mg Sod, 23 g Carb, 4 g Fib, 25 g Prot, 64 mg Calc. **POINTS** value: **4.**

GOOD IDEA Serve this zesty dish with baked tortilla chips and deduct them from your weekly **POINTS** Allowance (6 will increase the **POINTS** value by 1).

2 teaspoons olive oil

1 medium onion, chopped

2 garlic cloves, minced

1 green bell pepper, seeded and chopped

1 (14½-ounce) can diced tomatoes with mild green chiles

1 (10-ounce) box frozen corn kernels

¼ teaspoon salt

⅛ teaspoon cinnamon

1 pound skinless tilapia, orange roughy, or halibut fillets, cut into 1-inch pieces

2 tablespoons chopped fresh cilantro or parsley

4 lime wedges

Mahi Mahi with Mustard-Cognac Sauce

HANDS-ON PREP **5 MIN**
COOK **15 MIN**
SERVES **4**

1 Sprinkle the mahi mahi with the oregano, salt, and pepper. Heat the oil in a large nonstick skillet over medium-high heat. Add the mahi mahi and cook until golden on the outside and just opaque in the center, about 3 minutes on each side. Transfer the mahi mahi to a plate and cover lightly with foil to keep warm.

2 Add the shallots to the same skillet and cook over medium-high heat, stirring frequently, until golden, about 6 minutes. Add the cognac and cook, stirring frequently, about 30 seconds. Add the clam juice and mustard; bring to a simmer. Serve the sauce with the mahi mahi.

PER SERVING (1 piece mahi mahi and generous 2 tablespoons sauce): 153 Cal, 4 g Fat, 1 g Sat Fat, 0 g Trans Fat, 63 mg Chol, 551 mg Sod, 2 g Carb, 1 g Fib, 23 g Prot, 37 mg Calc. **_POINTS_** value: **_3._**

- 4 (¼-pound) pieces **mahi mahi fillets**
- 1 teaspoon **dried oregano**
- ½ teaspoon **salt**
- ¼ teaspoon **freshly ground pepper**
- 2 teaspoons **olive oil**
- 2 **shallots**, finely chopped
- 2 tablespoons **cognac**
- ½ cup bottled **clam juice** or **fish broth**
- 1 tablespoon **Dijon mustard**

**Parma-Wrapped Fillet of Sole
with Arugula**

Parma-Wrapped Fillet of Sole with Arugula

HANDS-ON PREP **10 MIN**
COOK **10 MIN**
SERVES **4**

1 Sprinkle the fillets evenly with the lemon juice and pepper. Top each fillet evenly with the arugula. Roll up the fillets and wrap each with a slice of prosciutto.

2 Melt the butter and oil in a large nonstick skillet over medium to medium-high heat. Add the fish rolls and cook, turning occasionally, until the fish is just opaque in the center and the prosciutto is lightly browned, about 8 minutes. Transfer the rolls to a warm platter. Add the wine to the skillet; cook, stirring to deglaze the pan, about 30 seconds. Drizzle the wine mixture over the fish rolls and serve with the lemon wedges.

PER SERVING (1 fish roll): 156 Cal, 6 g Fat, 2 g Sat Fat, 0 g Trans Fat, 65 mg Chol, 278 mg Sod, 1 g Carb, 0 g Fib, 22 g Prot, 27 mg Calc. *POINTS* value: *4.*

HOW WE DID IT To get clear pinwheel slices to eat, cut these with a serrated knife. Steamed yellow wax beans make a nice side to this dish.

4 (¼-pound) **skinless fillets of sole or flounder**

2 teaspoons **fresh lemon juice**

¼ teaspoon **freshly ground pepper**

1 **cup lightly packed arugula leaves**

4 **slices thinly sliced prosciutto (about 2 ounces) or Virginia baked ham**

2 teaspoons **butter**

2 teaspoons **olive oil**

2 tablespoons **dry white wine**

4 **lemon wedges**

Basil-Crusted Cod

HANDS-ON PREP **10 MIN**
COOK **10 MIN**
SERVES **4**

1 Preheat the oven to 500°F. Spray a 9-inch square baking dish with nonstick spray. Place the fish in the baking dish.

2 Combine the basil, onion, cornmeal, oil, lime juice, salt, and pepper in a small bowl. Spoon the mixture evenly on top of each piece of fish. Bake, uncovered, until the fish is just opaque in the center and lightly browned and crisp on top, about 10 minutes.

PER SERVING (1 piece cod): 225 Cal, 6 g Fat, 1 g Sat Fat, 0 g Trans Fat, 96 mg Chol, 445 mg Sod, 6 g Carb, 1 g Fib, 35 g Prot, 35 mg Calc. **POINTS** value: **5.**

HOW WE DID IT When buying fresh fish fillets or steaks, look for a fresh mild odor, firm-textured flesh that springs back when pressed with a finger, and a moist appearance.

¼ **pounds** cod or halibut fillet, **about** ½ **inch thick, cut into 4 pieces**

⅓ **cup finely chopped** fresh basil leaves

¼ **cup finely chopped** red onion

3 **tablespoons** cornmeal

1 **tablespoon** extra-virgin olive oil

2 **teaspoons** fresh lime juice

½ **teaspoon** salt

½ **teaspoon** freshly ground pepper

Broiled Red Snapper with Pesto Vinaigrette

HANDS-ON PREP **10 MIN**
COOK **10 MIN**
SERVES **4**

1 Spray the broiler rack with nonstick spray; preheat the broiler. Lightly spray both sides of the snapper, zucchini, radicchio, and onion with nonstick spray, then sprinkle with the salt and pepper.

2 Place the snapper, zucchini, and onion on the broiler rack; broil 4 inches from the heat until lightly browned, about 4 minutes. Turn the snapper, zucchini, and onion and add the radicchio to the broiler rack; broil 4 inches from the heat until the fish is just opaque in the center, the zucchini and onion are tender, and the radicchio is slightly wilted, about 4 minutes longer.

3 Meanwhile, combine the pesto and vinegar in a small bowl. Arrange the fish and vegetables on a large platter. Drizzle with the pesto and serve at once.

PER SERVING (1 fish fillet, ¼ of vegetables, and 1 tablespoon pesto): 208 Cal, 8 g Fat, 2 g Sat Fat, 0 g Trans Fat, 77 mg Chol, 520 mg Sod, 4 g Carb, 1 g Fib, 29 g Prot, 80 mg Calc.
POINTS value: **5.**

EXPRESS LANE Save time on cleanup—line the broiler pan with foil and lightly spray the foil with nonstick spray.

4 (4–5-ounce) skinless red snapper fillets

1 zucchini, cut into 4 lengthwise slices

1 small head radicchio, cut into 8 wedges

½ red onion, cut into 4 (¼-inch-thick) rounds

½ teaspoon salt

¼ teaspoon freshly ground pepper

3 tablespoons store-bought pesto

1 tablespoon white balsamic vinegar

Tilapia Seviche with Tomato and Orange

1 Combine the tilapia and lime juice in a medium bowl; toss to coat and set aside while preparing the other ingredients. Add the tomatoes, orange, onion, parsley, salt, and cayenne. Refrigerate, covered, about 10 minutes.

2 Arrange the Belgian endive leaves on a platter. Spoon the seviche evenly (scant ¼ cup) in the center of each leaf. Serve at once.

PER SERVING (3 pieces): 116 Cal, 1 g Fat, 0 g Sat Fat, 0 g Trans Fat, 45 mg Chol, 380 mg Sod, 9 g Carb, 3 g Fib, 17 g Prot, 48 mg Calc. **POINTS** value: **2.**

TRY IT Seviche (seh-VEE-che) is a delicious Latin American appetizer of super-fresh, raw fish marinated in citrus juice. It usually marinates for about 2 hours, but 10 minutes of marinating for this main dish is fine. Toss the fish with the lime juice first thing so it has a chance to turn opaque and use thin fillets such as tilapia, sole, or flounder and cut into small dice so the fish marinates quickly.

¾ **pound** very fresh tilapia, sole, or flounder fillets, **cut into ¼-inch pieces**

¼ **cup** fresh lime juice

12 grape tomatoes, cousely chopped

1 orange, peeled and diced

¼ **cup finely chopped** red onion

2 **tablespoons chopped** fresh parsley

½ **teaspoon** salt

⅛ **teaspoon** cayenne

12 **Belgian** endive leaves

Potato-Crusted Flounder with Tomato Salsa

HANDS-ON PREP **15 MIN**
COOK **5 MIN**
SERVES **4**

1 To make the salsa, combine the tomatoes, onion, cilantro, vinegar, and salt in a medium bowl.

2 Lightly beat the egg in a shallow dish. Place the potato flakes, Parmesan, and pepper on a sheet of wax paper. Dip each fillet into the egg then into the potato mixture, pressing gently so the flakes adhere.

3 Heat the oil in a large nonstick skillet over medium to medium-high heat. Add the fish and cook until browned on the outside and just opaque in the center, 2–3 minutes on each side. Serve the fish with the salsa.

PER SERVING (1 fish fillet and generous ¼ cup salsa): 205 Cal, 7 g Fat, 2 g Sat Fat, 0 g Trans Fat, 111 mg Chol, 322 mg Sod, 11 g Carb, 2 g Fib, 24 g Prot, 72 mg Calc. **POINTS** value: **4.**

FOOD NOTE Don't confuse potato flakes with instant mashed potatoes. The flakes are coarser in texture, which is necessary to properly coat the fish.

2 medium ripe tomatoes, chopped

½ small red onion, chopped

2 tablespoons chopped fresh cilantro or parsley

1 tablespoon white balsamic vinegar

¼ teaspoon salt

1 large egg

⅔ cup instant mashed potato flakes

2 tablespoons grated Parmesan cheese

½ teaspoon freshly ground pepper

4 (¼-pound) skinless flounder fillets

1 tablespoon olive oil

Curried Shrimp with Mango Sauce

HANDS-ON PREP **5 MIN**
COOK **10 MIN**
SERVES **4**

1 Combine the shrimp, curry powder, and salt in a medium bowl; stir until the shrimp are evenly coated. Let stand 5 minutes.

2 Meanwhile, puree the mango and water in a blender or food processor; set aside.

3 Heat the oil in a medium nonstick saucepan over medium-high heat. Add the onion, ginger, sugar, salt, and crushed red pepper; cook, stirring frequently, until lightly browned, about 3 minutes. Add the mango puree; bring to a boil, stirring occasionally. Reduce the heat and simmer about 1 minute.

4 Spray a large nonstick skillet with nonstick spray and set over medium-high heat. Add the shrimp and cook until browned on the outside and just opaque in the center, about 2 minutes on each side. Serve the shrimp with the sauce.

PER SERVING (about 7 shrimp and ⅓ cup sauce): 171 Cal, 4 g Fat, 1 g Sat Fat, 0 g Trans Fat, 161 mg Chol, 484 mg Sod, 17 g Carb, 2 g Fib, 18 g Prot, 53 mg Calc. *POINTS* value: *3.*

HOW WE DID IT Be sure to thoroughly pat the shrimp dry with paper towels before you coat them with the curry and salt. When cooking, arrange the shrimp in a single layer in the skillet, making sure they don't touch each other to prevent steaming.

1 **pound** peeled and deveined jumbo shrimp, **thawed if frozen**

1 **tablespoon** curry powder

¼ **teaspoon** salt

2 **cups (from a 24-ounce package)** frozen mango cubes, **thawed**

¼ **cup** water

2 **teaspoons** Asian (dark) sesame oil

1 small red onion, **finely chopped (about ½ cup)**

1 **tablespoon minced peeled** fresh ginger

1½ **teaspoons** sugar

¼ **teaspoon** salt

¼ **teaspoon** crushed red pepper

Thai Shrimp and Asparagus

Thai Shrimp and Asparagus

HANDS-ON PREP **10 MIN**
COOK **10 MIN**
SERVES **4**

1 Heat 1 teaspoon of the oil in a large nonstick skillet or wok over medium-high heat until a drop of water sizzles. Add the shrimp and garlic; stir-fry until the shrimp are just opaque in the center, about 3 minutes. Transfer to a plate.

2 Heat the remaining 1 teaspoon oil in the same skillet, then add the asparagus, bell pepper, and onion; stir-fry until crisp-tender, about 2 minutes. Add the ginger and curry paste; stir-fry until fragrant, about 30 seconds.

3 Add the coconut milk, fish sauce, and sugar; bring to a simmer. Cook, stirring frequently, about 3 minutes. Add the shrimp. Reduce the heat and simmer, stirring occasionally, until heated through, about 1 minute.

PER SERVING (about 1¼ cups): 203 Cal, 6 g Fat, 2 g Sat Fat, 0 g Trans Fat, 161 mg Chol, 750 mg Sod, 18 g Carb, 3 g Fib, 22 g Prot, 75 mg Calc. **POINTS** value: **4.**

EXPRESS LANE To save time, we use shrimp (either fresh or frozen) that is already peeled and deveined.

- 2 teaspoons canola oil
- 1 pound peeled and deveined large shrimp, thawed if frozen
- 2 garlic cloves, minced
- 1 (1-pound) bunch asparagus, trimmed and cut into 1½-inch pieces
- 1 orange bell pepper, seeded and cut into strips
- 1 onion, sliced
- 1 tablespoon grated peeled fresh ginger
- 1 teaspoon Thai red curry paste
- ½ cup light (reduced-fat) coconut milk
- 1½ tablespoons Asian fish sauce (nam pla)
- 1 tablespoon packed brown sugar

Shrimp and Cremini Mushroom Frittata

HANDS-ON PREP **5 MIN**
COOK **12 MIN**
SERVES **6**

1 Heat the oil in a large nonstick skillet over medium-high heat. Add the scallions, mushrooms, zucchini, salt, and pepper. Cook, stirring frequently, until the vegetables are softened and golden, about 6 minutes. Stir in the shrimp and basil.

2 Reduce the heat to medium and pour the egg substitute over the vegetables and shrimp. Cook until set, lifting the edges frequently with a spatula to let the uncooked egg flow underneath, about 3 minutes.

3 Sprinkle the cheese over the frittata. Cover the skillet; reduce the heat to low and cook until the cheese melts, about 3 minutes. Cut into 6 wedges.

PER SERVING (1 wedge): 127 Cal, 4 g Fat, 1 g Sat Fat, 0 g Trans Fat, 59 mg Chol, 464 mg Sod, 4 g Carb, 1 g Fib, 18 g Prot, 119 mg Calc. **POINTS** value: **3.**

GOOD IDEA If you feel you need just a little something more, serve this frittata with breadsticks and deduct them from your weekly **POINTS Allowance** (2 long breadsticks will increase the **POINTS** value by 1).

1 tablespoon canola oil

4 scallions, sliced

¼ pound fresh cremini or baby bella mushrooms, chopped

1 small zucchini, diced (¾ cup)

½ teaspoon salt

¼ teaspoon freshly ground pepper

½ pound cooked small shrimp

2 tablespoons chopped fresh basil

2 cups fat-free egg substitute

½ cup shredded fat-free mozzarella cheese

Moroccan Scallops

HANDS-ON PREP **5 MIN**
COOK **15 MIN**
SERVES **4**

1 Heat the oil in a large nonstick skillet over medium-high heat. Add the onion, garlic, ginger, coriander, and cayenne. Cook, stirring frequently, until softened and fragrant, about 3 minutes. Add the bell pepper and cook, stirring occasionally, until softened, about 3 minutes.

2 Add the clam juice, lemon juice, raisins, and salt to the skillet; bring to a boil. Reduce the heat and simmer, uncovered, about 5 minutes.

3 Add the scallops, spooning some of the liquid over them and simmer, covered, until just opaque in the center, about 5 minutes. Stir in the parsley, just before serving.

PER SERVING (6 scallops with ½ cup broth and vegetables): 136 Cal, 3 g Fat, 0 g Sat Fat, 0 g Trans Fat, 32 mg Chol, 580 mg Sod, 13 g Carb, 1 g Fib, 14 g Prot, 98 mg Calc. **POINTS** value: **3.**

GOOD IDEA Keep with North African tradition and serve this with couscous and sprinkle with sliced almonds (½ cup cooked couscous will increase the **POINTS** value by 1½, and ½ tablespoon sliced almonds will increase the **POINTS** value by ½).

2 teaspoons olive oil

1 onion, chopped

2 garlic cloves, minced

½ teaspoon ground ginger

½ teaspoon ground coriander or cinnamon

⅛ teaspoon cayenne

1 yellow bell pepper, seeded and chopped

1 (8-ounce) bottle clam juice, or 1 cup fish or vegetable broth

1 tablespoon fresh lemon juice

¼ cup golden raisins

½ teaspoon salt

1 pound sea scallops (about 24 to the pound)

¼ cup chopped fresh parsley

Scallop Miso Bowl with Soba Noodles and Spinach

HANDS-ON PREP **5 MIN**
COOK **15 MIN**
SERVES **4**

1 Heat the oil in a Dutch oven over medium heat. Add the garlic and ginger; cook, stirring constantly, until fragrant, about 1 minute. Add the broth, miso, and cayenne; bring to a boil. Add the soba noodles; return to a boil. Cook over medium heat, stirring occasionally, until the noodles are partially cooked, about 3 minutes.

2 Add the scallops and spinach; return to a boil and simmer until the scallops are just opaque in the center and the noodles are cooked, about 4 minutes. Serve the soup, sprinkled with the scallions.

PER SERVING (6 scallops with 1 cup broth and noodles): 293 Cal, 5 g Fat, 1 g Sat Fat, 0 g Trans Fat, 39 mg Chol, 1146 mg Sod, 40 g Carb, 5 g Fib, 23 g Prot, 172 mg Calc. *POINTS* value: *5.*

EXPRESS LANE Save time and use 1 teaspoon ground ginger instead of grating fresh ginger.

2 teaspoons Asian (dark) sesame oil

2 garlic cloves, minced

1 tablespoon minced peeled fresh ginger

5 cups fish or vegetable broth or bottled clam juice

2 tablespoons miso

Pinch cayenne

6 ounces soba noodles or thin spaghetti

1 pound sea scallops (about 24 to the pound)

1 (6-ounce) bag baby spinach leaves

3 scallions, thinly sliced

Scallop Miso Bowl with
Soba Noodles and Spinach

Crab and Spinach Quesadillas

Crab and Spinach Quesadillas

HANDS-ON PREP **10 MIN**
COOK **10 MIN**
SERVES **4**

1 Preheat the oven to 500°F. Spray a large nonstick baking sheet with nonstick spray.

2 Heat the oil in a large nonstick skillet over medium-high heat. Add the onion, and cook, stirring occasionally, until golden, about 3 minutes. Add the spinach and cook, stirring, until wilted, about 1 minute. Remove from the heat and stir in the crabmeat.

3 Place the tortillas on a work surface. Top one-half of each tortilla with 2 tablespoons of the cheese, one-fourth of the crabmeat mixture, then 2 tablespoons more of the cheese. Fold the top halves of the tortillas over the filling to form semi circles, lightly pressing the edges to seal, making 4 quesadillas.

4 Place the quesadillas on the baking sheet; spray the tops of the quesadillas lightly with nonstick spray and bake until lightly browned and the cheese melts, about 3 minutes on each side.

PER SERVING (1 quesadilla): 207 Cal, 6 g Fat, 2 g Sat Fat, 0 g Trans Fat, 44 mg Chol, 590 mg Sod, 20 g Carb, 3 g Fib, 19 g Prot, 274 mg Calc. **POINTS** value: **4.**

GOOD IDEA If you don't want to turn your oven on, cook the quesadillas in a skillet, which has been sprayed with nonstick spray, over medium heat for about 3 minutes on each side. Most skillets will hold 2 quesadillas at a time.

2 teaspoons olive oil

1 onion, thinly sliced

2 cups packed baby spinach or arugula leaves

1 (6-ounce) can crabmeat, drained

4 (8-inch) whole-wheat flour tortillas

1 cup shredded reduced-fat pepperjack cheese

Crabmeat Salad

HANDS-ON PREP **20 MIN**
COOK **NONE**
SERVES **4**

1 Combine the crabmeat, bell pepper, fennel, scallions, mayonnaise, dill, capers, and lemon juice in a bowl; mix well.

2 Arrange the lettuce on each of 4 plates. Spoon about ¾ cup of the crabmeat salad onto each and serve at once.

PER SERVING (1 plate): 118 Cal, 6 g Fat, 1 g Sat Fat, 0 g Trans Fat, 58 mg Chol, 369 mg Sod, 5 g Carb, 1 g Fib, 12 g Prot, 77 mg Calc. *POINTS* value: *3.*

PLAY IT SAFE You can buy convenient containers of pasteurized crabmeat in the refrigerated section of the supermarket's fish department. Pasteurized crabmeat has been heated to kill any organisms that might be present. You can keep it, refrigerated, for as long as the sell-by date. Once you open the package, however, plan to use it within a day or two, as you would fresh crabmeat.

½ **pound** cooked lump crabmeat, picked over for pieces of shell, or 1 (8-ounce) container pasteurized crabmeat

1 small red bell pepper, seeded and chopped

⅓ cup finely chopped fennel or celery

3 scallions, chopped

¼ cup low-fat mayonnaise

¼ cup chopped fresh dill

2 tablespoons drained capers

1½ tablespoons fresh lemon juice

4 leafy green lettuce leaves

New England Lobster Sandwiches

HANDS-ON PREP **15 MIN**
COOK **NONE**
SERVES **4**

1 Combine the mayonnaise, onion, lemon juice, mustard, and cayenne in a medium bowl. Add the lobster and celery; mix well.

2 Spread one-fourth of the lobster mixture (a scant ½ cup) on each of 4 slices of the bread. Top with the remaining 4 slices of bread. Serve at once.

PER SERVING (1 sandwich): 228 Cal, 6 g Fat, 1 g Sat Fat, 0 g Trans Fat, 37 mg Chol, 620 mg Sod, 29 g Carb, 4 g Fib, 15 g Prot, 76 mg Calc. *POINTS* value: *4.*

HOW WE DID IT Frozen lobster comes in big chunks, so we snip them into smaller chunks with a scissor.

3 tablespoons low-fat mayonnaise

2 tablespoons finely chopped red onion

1 tablespoon fresh lemon juice

2 teaspoons Dijon mustard

⅛ teaspoon cayenne

1 (7-ounce) container fully cooked frozen lobster meat, thawed and drained

1 celery stalk, finely chopped

8 slices (3 x 5 inches) crusty whole-wheat bread, toasted

Mussels in Spicy Tomato Sauce with Fresh Linguine

HANDS-ON PREP **5 MIN**
COOK **15 MIN**
SERVES **4**

1 Fill a large saucepan with 2 quarts water and bring it to a boil over high heat.

2 Meanwhile, heat the oil in a nonstick Dutch oven over medium-high heat. Add the onion and garlic; cook, stirring occasionally, until golden, about 7 minutes. Add the tomatoes, wine, and crushed red pepper; bring to a boil. Reduce the heat and simmer about 2 minutes.

3 Add the mussels, spooning the sauce over them. Cover the Dutch oven and simmer until the mussels open, about 5 minutes. Discard any mussels that do not open. Stir in the basil and parsley.

4 When the water boils, add the linguine and cook until just al dente, according to package directions. Drain and toss immediately with about ½ cup of the sauce from the Dutch oven, then turn onto a heated platter. Top with the remaining sauce and mussels and serve at once.

PER SERVING (2 cups mussels in shells and ¾ cup pasta with sauce): 391 Cal, 6 g Fat, 1 g Sat Fat, 0 g Trans Fat, 22 mg Chol, 356 mg Sod, 61 g Carb, 6 g Fib, 19 g Prot, 108 mg Calc. *POINTS* value: **8.**

HOW WE DID IT After buying mussels, discard those with broken shells or shells that do not close tightly when gently tapped. The hairy filaments that protrude from a mussel are known as a "beard." To remove, pinch the filaments between thumb and forefinger and pull firmly. Some mussels available today have no beards.

1 tablespoon extra-virgin olive oil

1 onion, chopped

5 garlic cloves, minced

1 (14½-ounce) can diced tomatoes

½ cup dry white wine

¼ teaspoon crushed red pepper

2 pounds mussels, scrubbed and debearded

¼ cup chopped fresh basil

¼ cup chopped flat-leaf parsley

1 (9-ounce) package fresh linguine

Mussels in Spicy Tomato Sauce with Fresh Linguine

Clams Capellini with Fresh Tomatoes

HANDS-ON PREP **5 MIN**
COOK **15 MIN**
SERVES **4**

1 Fill a large saucepan with 2 quarts water and bring it to a boil over high heat.

2 Meanwhile, heat the oil in a large nonstick skillet over medium heat. Add the garlic and cook, stirring constantly, until fragrant, about 1 minute. Add the clams and their juice; bring to a boil and cook rapidly until the liquid is reduced by about half, about 2 minutes. Add the wine, tomatoes, parsley, basil, and pepper; return to a boil. Reduce the heat and simmer 1 minute.

3 When the water boils, add the capellini and cook until tender, about 2 minutes. Drain and toss immediately with the clam mixture.

PER SERVING (scant 1 cup): 382 Cal, 6 g Fat, 1 g Sat Fat, 0 g Trans Fat, 47 mg Chol, 98 mg Sod, 52 g Carb, 4 g Fib, 26 g Prot, 100 mg Calc. **POINTS** value: **7.**

FOOD NOTE If you have an extra 3 or 4 minutes, you can cook traditional linguine instead of capellini to go with this delicious clam sauce.

1 tablespoon olive oil

2 garlic cloves, minced

1 (10-ounce) can baby clams, undrained

3 tablespoons dry white wine

2 plum tomatoes, chopped

⅓ cup chopped fresh parsley

1 tablespoon chopped fresh basil or 1 teaspoon dried

¼ teaspoon freshly ground pepper

½ pound capellini or angel hair pasta

Easy Bouillabaisse with Spinach

HANDS-ON PREP **5 MIN**
COOK **15 MIN**
SERVES **4**

1 Heat the oil in a large nonstick Dutch oven over high heat. Add the onion, bell pepper, and garlic; cook, stirring occasionally, until softened and lightly browned, about 4 minutes. Add the clam juice, tomatoes, wine, thyme, and pepper; bring to a boil over high heat.

2 Add the fish fillets, shrimp, and mussels; return to a boil over high heat, stirring occasionally. Reduce the heat and simmer, covered, until the fish and shrimp are just opaque in the center and the mussels open, about 2 minutes. Discard any mussels that don't open. Stir in the spinach until wilted, about 1 minute.

PER SERVING (about 2 cups): 186 Cal, 5 g Fat, 1 g Sat Fat, 0 g Trans Fat, 122 mg Chol, 740 mg Sod, 11 g Carb, 3 g Fib, 24 g Prot, 118 mg Calc. **_POINTS_** value: **_4._**

HOW WE DID IT Since mussels can be sandy, soak them in a bowl of cold water for 2 to 3 minutes. Repeat, using fresh water until there is no more sand in the bowl. Then scrub them with a stiff brush under cold running water.

1 tablespoon olive oil

1 cup frozen chopped onions

½ cup frozen chopped green bell pepper

1 large garlic clove, minced

3 (8-ounce) bottles clam juice, or 3 cups fish or vegetable broth

1 (14½-ounce) can diced tomatoes

¼ cup dry white wine

1 teaspoon dried thyme

¼ teaspoon coarsely ground black pepper

½ pound skinless fish fillets, such as halibut or cod, cut into 1-inch pieces

½ pound medium peeled and deveined shrimp

½ pound scrubbed mussels

2 cups baby spinach leaves

Hearty Vegetarian Main Dishes

p 151

p 165

p 168

CHAPTER 6

Coconut Curried Tofu

Coconut Curried Tofu

HANDS-ON PREP **10 MIN**
COOK **10 MIN**
SERVES **4**

1 Stir together the coconut milk, fish sauce, honey, cornstarch, and curry paste in a small bowl until smooth; set aside.

2 Heat 1½ teaspoons of the oil in a large nonstick skillet over high heat. Add the tofu and cook, stirring often, until lightly golden, about 4 minutes; transfer to a bowl.

3 Heat the remaining 1½ teaspoons oil in the same skillet. Add the asparagus, bell pepper, water, and ginger; cook, stirring constantly, until the liquid evaporates and the vegetables are crisp-tender, about 3 minutes. Add the tofu and coconut milk mixture. Cook, stirring constantly, until thickened, about 1 minute. Serve sprinkled with the cilantro.

PER SERVING (1 cup): 157 Cal, 7 g Fat, 3 g Sat Fat, 0 g Trans Fat, 0 mg Chol, 457 mg Sod, 18 g Carb, 3 g Fib, 11 g Prot, 67 mg Calc. **POINTS** value: **3.**

FOOD NOTE Spicy Thai curry paste adds both heat and tang, balancing the sweetness of the coconut and the honey in this recipe. If you'd like your food hotter, add a little more curry paste—but be careful not to let it overwhelm the dish.

¾ **cup light (reduced-fat) coconut milk**

1 tablespoon **fish sauce (nam pla)**

1 tablespoon **honey**

2 teaspoons **cornstarch**

¼ teaspoon **Thai red curry paste**

3 teaspoons **peanut oil**

1 (14-ounce) **package low-fat firm tofu, drained and cut into ½-inch cubes**

1 **pound** fresh **asparagus, trimmed and cut into 1½-inch pieces**

1 **red bell pepper, seeded and cut into strips**

¼ cup **water**

1 tablespoon **grated fresh ginger**

2 tablespoons **chopped fresh cilantro (optional)**

Tofu Lo Mein

HANDS-ON PREP **10 MIN**
COOK **10 MIN**
SERVES **6**

1 Cook the noodles according to package directions; drain and keep warm.

2 Meanwhile, stir together the broth, sake, soy sauce, honey, and cornstarch in a small bowl until smooth; set aside.

3 Heat a large nonstick skillet or wok over high heat until a drop of water sizzles. Pour in 2 teaspoons of the oil and swirl to coat the pan. Add the tofu and stir-fry until lightly golden, about 4 minutes. Transfer the tofu to a bowl.

4 Heat the remaining 2 teaspoons oil in the wok. Add the snow peas, mushrooms, scallions, and garlic; stir-fry until crisp-tender, about 4 minutes. Add the broth mixture and cook, stirring constantly, until thickened, about 1 minute. Add the reserved noodles and tofu; heat through, tossing gently, about 1 minute.

PER SERVING (1 cup): 255 Cal, 4 g Fat, 1 g Sat Fat, 0 g Trans Fat, 0 mg Chol, 603 mg Sod, 42 g Carb, 4 g Fib, 11 g Prot, 58 mg Calc. **POINTS** value: **5.**

FOOD NOTE Quick-cooking lo mein noodles—available in most supermarkets—make this stir-fry extra easy; substitute thin spaghetti if it's unavailable.

8 ounces **lo mein noodles**

¾ cup **vegetable broth**

3 tablespoons **sake**

3 tablespoons **reduced-sodium soy sauce**

1½ tablespoons **honey**

1 tablespoon **cornstarch**

4 teaspoons **Asian (dark) sesame oil**

1 (14-ounce) container **low-fat firm tofu, drained and cut into ½-inch pieces**

1 (6-ounce) bag **ready-to-use fresh snow peas**

1 cup sliced **fresh white mushrooms (about 3 ounces)**

5 **scallions**, trimmed and cut into ¾-inch pieces

3 **garlic cloves**, minced

Tuscan "Pitzas"

HANDS-ON PREP **5 MIN**
COOK **8 MIN**
SERVES **4**

1 Preheat the oven to 425°F. Spray a baking sheet with nonstick spray.

2 Combine the beans, lemon juice, oil, sage, and pepper in a medium bowl. Mix well with a wooden spoon, partially mashing the beans as you stir.

3 Spread each pita with ¼ of the bean mixture, ¼ cup of the ricotta cheese, 6 tomato halves, and 1 tablespoon of the Parmesan cheese. Place on the baking sheet and bake until hot and the pitas are crisp, about 8 minutes.

PER SERVING (1 pitza): 366 Cal, 6 g Fat, 2 g Sat Fat, 0 g Trans Fat, 11 mg Chol, 443 mg Sod, 55 g Carb, 7 g Fib, 23 g Prot, 301 mg Calc. **POINTS** value: **7.**

EXPRESS LANE If you want to get a jump start on dinner, the pitzas can be assembled up to 3 hours ahead and stored in the refrigerator covered with plastic wrap. When you bake them add a couple of extra minutes to allow the pitas to crisp.

1 (15½-ounce) can cannellini (white kidney) beans, rinsed and drained

2 tablespoons fresh lemon juice

1 tablespoon extra-virgin olive oil

1 tablespoon chopped fresh sage

¼ teaspoon freshly ground pepper

4 (6-inch) pitas

1 cup fat-free ricotta cheese

12 cherry tomatoes, halved

¼ cup freshly grated Parmesan cheese

Meatless Fettuccine Bolognese

HANDS-ON PREP **5 MIN**
COOK **10 MIN**
SERVES **4**

1 Cook the fettuccine according to package directions; drain and keep warm.

2 Meanwhile, heat the oil in a large nonstick skillet over medium-high heat. Add the onion and garlic; cook, stirring, until softened, about 4 minutes. Stir in the soy crumbles and heat through, about 3 minutes. Reduce the heat and add the tomato sauce; cook until hot and bubbling, about 3 minutes. Remove from the heat and stir in the cheese and pepper.

3 Divide the pasta among 4 bowls, and top evenly with the sauce.

PER SERVING (1 cup fettuccine and ¾ cup sauce): 370 Cal, 8 g Fat, 2 g Sat Fat, 0 g Trans Fat, 48 mg Chol, 753 mg Sod, 45 g Carb, 3 g Fib, 29 g Prot, 179 mg Calc. **_POINTS_** value: 7.

EXPRESS LANE This sauce is easily doubled and great to have on hand for quick pasta dinners. Prepare the sauce ahead of time and refrigerate for up to 3 days, or freeze in freezer containers for up to 3 months. Thaw it overnight in the refrigerator, then reheat in a saucepan over medium-high heat.

- 1 (9-ounce) package fresh fettuccine
- 1 tablespoon extra-virgin olive oil
- 1 medium onion, chopped
- 3 garlic cloves, minced
- 2 cups frozen soy protein crumbles
- 2 cups (from a 26-ounce jar) fat-free garlic-herb tomato sauce
- ⅓ cup freshly grated Parmesan cheese
- ¼ teaspoon freshly ground pepper

Meatless Fettuccine Bolognese

Macaroni and Cheese

Macaroni and Cheese

HANDS-ON PREP **5 MIN**
COOK **15 MIN**
SERVES **4**

1 Cook the macaroni according to package directions; drain and keep warm.

2 Meanwhile, whisk together the milk and cornstarch in a small bowl; set aside.

3 Melt the butter in a large nonstick saucepan over medium-high heat. Add the onion and cook, stirring occasionally, until slightly softened, about 3 minutes. Add the mustard and pepper; cook 30 seconds more. Stir in the milk mixture and cook, stirring constantly, until thickened, about 3 minutes. Add the cheese and cook, stirring, just until melted. Stir in the macaroni and tomatoes and heat through, about 1 minute. Serve at once.

PER SERVING (1¼ cups): 322 Cal, 5 g Fat, 2 g Sat Fat, 0 g Trans Fat, 12 mg Chol, 703 mg Sod, 50 g Carb, 4 g Fib, 19 g Prot, 404 mg Calc. **POINTS** value: **6.**

GOOD IDEA For a spicy Mexican variation, stir in 1 finely chopped chipotle pepper in adobo sauce when you add the cheese, and add 1 tablespoon chopped cilantro with the tomatoes. You'll find canned chipotles in adobo—smoked, dried jalapeño peppers in a complex, garlicky sauce—in Mexican groceries and some supermarkets. For a quick 1-*POINT* value-per-serving topping, grate a slice of whole-wheat bread, toss with 2 teaspoons melted butter, and sprinkle evenly over each serving.

1½ cups **elbow macaroni**

1½ cups **fat-free milk**

1 tablespoon **cornstarch**

1 teaspoon **unsalted butter**

1 **small onion, chopped**

1 teaspoon **dry mustard**

¼ teaspoon **freshly ground pepper**

1¼ cups shredded **extra-sharp reduced-fat cheddar cheese**

1 (14½-ounce) can **diced tomatoes, drained**

Blue Cheese Polenta with Sautéed Onions

HANDS-ON PREP **10 MIN**
COOK **10 MIN**
SERVES **6**

1 Melt the butter in a large nonstick skillet over high heat. Add the onions, sugar, ¼ teaspoon of the salt, and the cayenne; cook, stirring occasionally, until lightly golden, about 10 minutes.

2 Meanwhile, combine the milk, water, the remaining ¾ teaspoon salt, and the pepper in a medium saucepan over high heat; bring to a boil. Whisk in the polenta in a slow steady stream, and cook, whisking constantly, until thick and smooth, about 5 minutes. Remove from the heat and stir in the blue and Neufchâtel cheeses until melted and smooth. Serve with the sautéed onions.

PER SERVING (¾ cup polenta and about ¼ cup onions): 285 Cal, 11 g Fat, 7 g Sat Fat, 0 g Trans Fat, 30 mg Chol, 734 mg Sod, 36 g Carb, 2 g Fib, 12 g Prot, 265 mg Calc. **POINTS** value: **6.**

FOOD NOTE If you prefer, you can sauté or grill the polenta. Proceed with the recipe as directed, reducing the milk to 2 cups and the water to 1 cup. After cooking, press the polenta into a 9 x 13-inch baking pan that has been sprayed with nonstick spray, cover with plastic wrap, and refrigerate until firm, about 1 hour. Remove from the pan and cut into squares, rectangles, or triangles. Brush both sides lightly with olive oil and sauté in a nonstick skillet or grill until golden, about 2 minutes on each side.

1 tablespoon **unsalted butter**

4 **yellow onions, sliced**

1 tablespoon **sugar**

1 teaspoon **salt**

⅛ teaspoon **cayenne**

3 cups **low-fat (1%) milk**

2 cups **water**

¼ teaspoon **freshly ground pepper**

1 cup **quick-cooking polenta**

¾ cup **crumbled blue cheese**

2 ounces **light cream cheese (Neufchâtel)**

Orzo "Risotto" with Asparagus, Tomatoes, and Cheese

HANDS-ON PREP **5 MIN**
COOK **15 MIN**
SERVES **4**

1 Cook the orzo according to package directions, adding the asparagus during the last 2 minutes of cooking time. Drain and keep warm.

2 Meanwhile, heat the oil in a large nonstick skillet over medium-high heat. Add the onion and garlic; cook, stirring, until the onion is slightly softened, about 2 minutes. Add the tomatoes and cook until just wilted, about 2 minutes. Stir in the reserved orzo and asparagus and heat through, about 2 minutes more. Remove the skillet from the heat and stir in the ricotta and Parmesan cheeses, the basil, salt, and pepper.

PER SERVING (1¼ cups): 284 Cal, 7 g Fat, 2 g Sat Fat, 0 g Trans Fat, 11 mg Chol, 589 mg Sod, 39 g Carb, 5 g Fib, 19 g Prot, 229 mg Calc. **POINTS** value: **5.**

HOW WE DID IT Be sure to use a good quality, freshly grated Parmesan cheese, such as Parmigiano-Reggiano, in this dish. It will add an extra depth of flavor to the orzo without excessive fat or calories.

- 1 cup orzo
- 1 pound fresh asparagus, trimmed and cut into 1-inch pieces
- 1 tablespoon extra-virgin olive oil
- 1 onion, chopped
- 3 garlic cloves, minced
- 2 plum tomatoes, chopped
- 1 cup fat-free ricotta cheese
- ¼ cup freshly grated Parmesan cheese
- ¼ cup coarsely chopped fresh basil
- ½ teaspoon salt
- ¼ teaspoon freshly ground pepper

Gnocchi with Parsley Pesto

HANDS-ON PREP **5 MIN**
COOK **10 MIN**
SERVES **4**

1 Cook the gnocchi according to package directions; drain and keep warm.

2 Meanwhile to make the pesto sauce, put the parsley, basil, cheese, oil, anchovy, capers, garlic, salt, and pepper in a blender and process on high speed until smooth, about 2 minutes. Stop to scrape down the sides of the blender once. Toss the gnocchi with the pesto and serve at once.

PER SERVING (¾ cup): 287 Cal, 9 g Fat, 2 g Sat Fat, 0 g Trans Fat, 4 mg Chol, 892 mg Sod, 52 g Carb, 2 g Fib, 7 g Prot, 102 mg Calc. **POINTS** value: **6.**

TRY IT *Gnocchi* (NYOK-kee) are bite-size pasta dumplings, made primarily from flour and potatoes. When fresh, they cook in mere seconds; find them in the fresh pasta section of your supermarket. If unavailable, you can substitute 3 cups of frozen gnocchi, prepared according to package directions.

1 (17½-ounce) package fresh gnocchi

¾ cup chopped flat-leaf parsley

¾ cup chopped fresh basil

3 tablespoons freshly grated Parmesan cheese

2 tablespoons extra-virgin olive oil

1 anchovy fillet, rinsed and patted dry

1 teaspoon drained capers

1 garlic clove

½ teaspoon salt

¼ teaspoon freshly ground pepper

Gnocchi with Parsley Pesto

Tomato, Basil, and Ricotta Omelette

HANDS-ON PREP **5 MIN**
COOK **10 MIN**
SERVES **4**

1 Lightly beat the eggs, egg whites, ½ teaspoon of the salt, and ⅛ teaspoon of the pepper in a medium bowl; set aside.

2 Heat 2 teaspoons of the oil in a large nonstick skillet over high heat. Add the onion, garlic, basil, and the remaining ¼ teaspoon salt and ⅛ teaspoon pepper; cook, stirring occasionally, until the onion softens, about 2 minutes. Add the tomato; cook until wilted, about 2 minutes. Transfer to a bowl and stir in the ricotta and mozzarella cheeses.

3 Wipe out the skillet with a paper towel and return it to high heat; add the remaining 2 teaspoons oil. Pour in the egg mixture and cook, lifting the edges frequently with a spatula to allow the uncooked egg to flow underneath, until the eggs are just set, about 3 minutes. Spoon the cheese mixture over half of the eggs; folding the eggs over with a spatula to enclose the filling. Cook, turning once, until the filling is heated through, about 2 minutes. Cut the omelette in to 4 pieces and serve at once.

PER SERVING (¼ of omelette): 177 Cal, 10 g Fat, 2 g Sat Fat, 0 g Trans Fat, 215 mg Chol, 658 mg Sod, 7 g Carb, 1 g Fib, 14 g Prot, 128 mg Calc. **POINTS** value: **4.**

FOOD NOTE To make individual omelettes, use 1 large egg and 1 egg white beaten with ⅛ teaspoon salt and a pinch of pepper, then divide the cheese filling into fourths. Spray a small nonstick skillet with cooking spray, and proceed with the recipe as directed, allowing 1 to 2 minutes for the eggs to set.

4 large eggs

4 egg whites

¾ **teaspoon** salt

¼ **teaspoon** freshly ground pepper

4 teaspoons extra-virgin olive oil

1 medium onion, chopped

2 garlic cloves, minced

1 teaspoon dried basil

1 plum tomato, chopped

¼ **cup** fat-free ricotta cheese

¼ **cup** shredded fat-free mozzarella cheese

Cuban Black Beans and Rice

HANDS-ON PREP **5 MIN**
COOK **10 MIN**
SERVES **4**

1 Prepare the rice according to package directions, omitting the salt; keep warm.

2 Meanwhile, heat the oil in a large saucepan over high heat. Add the onion, red and green bell peppers, the garlic, vinegar, oregano, and coriander; cook, stirring, until the vegetables soften, about 5 minutes. Stir in the beans and their liquid. Reduce the heat and simmer, covered, until the sauce thickens slightly, about 5 minutes. Serve over the rice.

PER SERVING (scant ½ cup rice and ¾ cup beans): 301 Cal, 5 g Fat, 1 g Sat Fat, 0 g Trans Fat, 0 mg Chol, 337 mg Sod, 48 g Carb, 10 g Fib, 11 g Prot, 90 mg Calc. *POINTS* value: **6.**

FOOD NOTE Select canned organic black beans, if possible; they tend to be firmer and have much less sodium than the more widely distributed commercial brands.

¾ **cup quick-cooking brown rice**

1 **tablespoon** extra-virgin olive oil

1 **onion,** chopped

1 **red bell pepper, seeded and chopped**

1 **green bell pepper, seeded and chopped**

4 **garlic cloves,** minced

1 **tablespoon** sherry vinegar

1 **teaspoon** dried oregano

1 **teaspoon** ground coriander

1 **(15½-ounce) can black beans, undrained**

Escarole with Beans and Pasta

Escarole with Beans and Pasta

HANDS-ON PREP **10 MIN**
COOK **10 MIN**
SERVES **4**

1 Cook the cavatelli according to package directions omitting the salt; drain and keep warm.

2 Meanwhile, heat the oil in a large nonstick skillet over medium-high heat. Add the garlic and crushed red pepper; cook, stirring constantly, until fragrant, about 30 seconds. Add the escarole, a handful at a time, stirring until it has all been incorporated. Add the chickpeas and cook, stirring, until the escarole is wilted, about 2 minutes. Add the broth and salt; bring to a simmer. Cook, uncovered, until the broth is slightly reduced, about 4 minutes. Add the pasta and heat through, about 1 minute. Remove from the heat and stir in the cheese. Serve at once.

PER SERVING (1 cup): 374 Cal, 8 g Fat, 2 g Sat Fat, 0 g Trans Fat, 7 mg Chol, 779 mg Sod, 60 g Carb, 11 g Fib, 16 g Prot, 189 mg Calc. **POINTS** value: **7.**

FOOD NOTE No cavatelli in your supermarket freezer? Substitute 3 cups of any cooked medium-size pasta, such as shells, ziti, rotini, radiatore, or farfalle (bow ties).

8 ounces frozen cavatelli

1 tablespoon extra-virgin olive oil

6 garlic cloves, sliced

⅛ teaspoon crushed red pepper

1 pound fresh escarole, trimmed and cut into 2-inch pieces

1 (15½-ounce) can chickpeas, rinsed and drained

1 cup vegetable broth

¼ teaspoon salt

¼ cup freshly grated Romano cheese

Three-Bean Panzanella Salad

HANDS-ON PREP **15 MIN**
COOK **NONE**
SERVES **12**

Whisk together the vinegar, oil, and pepper in a large bowl. Add the bread, onion, cucumber, tomatoes, the cannellini, black, and red kidney beans, the cheese and basil; toss well to coat.

PER SERVING (generous 1 cup): 214 Cal, 5 g Fat, 1 g Sat Fat, 0 g Trans Fat, 3 mg Chol, 401 mg Sod, 32 g Carb, 6 g Fib, 11 g Prot, 117 mg Calc. **POINTS** value: **4.**

FOOD NOTE This salad is big enough to serve a crowd, but it's also delightful as leftovers. Store extras in the refrigerator for up to 3 days.

⅓ **cup balsamic vinegar**

3 **tablespoons extra-virgin olive oil**

½ **teaspoon freshly ground pepper**

8 **ounces sturdy Italian bread, cut into ½-inch cubes**

1 **red onion, thinly sliced**

1 **cucumber, peeled, halved lengthwise, seeded, and cut into ¼-inch-thick slices**

1 **pint cherry tomatoes, halved**

1 **(15½-ounce) can cannellini (white kidney) beans, rinsed and drained**

1 **(15½-ounce) can black beans, rinsed and drained**

1 **(15½-ounce) can red kidney beans, rinsed and drained**

¾ **cup reduced-fat feta cheese**

¼ **cup chopped fresh basil**

Hummus Bruschetta with Mediterranean Salad

HANDS-ON PREP **10 MIN**
COOK **7 MIN**
SERVES **4**

1 Preheat the oven to 425°F.

2 Arrange the bread slices in a single layer on a baking sheet; bake until lightly golden and crisp, about 7 minutes. Let cool.

3 Meanwhile, to make the hummus, put the chickpeas, water, lemon juice and zest, the oil, and garlic in a food processor and pulse until smooth, about 2 minutes. Spread each bread slice with 1 tablespoon of the hummus; set aside.

4 Toss together the tomatoes, cucumber, artichoke hearts, scallions, olives, and dressing in a large bowl. Divide among 4 plates and serve with the bruschetta.

PER SERVING (1 cup salad with 4 bruschetta): 309 Cal, 9 g Fat, 1 g Sat Fat, 0 g Trans Fat, 0 mg Chol, 596 mg Sod, 47 g Carb, 10 g Fib, 12 g Prot, 104 mg Calc. **POINTS** value: **6.**

GOOD IDEA For more authentic flavor in your hummus, add 2 tablespoons of tahini (creamy sesame paste found in the ethnic food section of most supermarkets) to the hummus and increase the **POINTS** value per serving by 1.

4 ounces Italian bread, cut into 16 slices

1 (15½-ounce) can chickpeas, rinsed and drained

¼ cup water

Juice and grated zest of 1 lemon

1½ tablespoons extra-virgin olive oil

1 garlic clove

1 pint cherry tomatoes, quartered

1 small cucumber, peeled, seeded, and coarsely chopped

1 (8½-ounce) can quartered artichoke hearts, drained and coarsely chopped

2 scallions, chopped

3 tablespoons drained chopped olives

2 tablespoons fat-free Italian dressing

Couscous-Stuffed Tomatoes

HANDS-ON PREP **5 MIN**
COOK **10 MIN**
SERVES **6**

1 Bring the water, ¼ teaspoon of the salt, and ⅛ teaspoon of the pepper to a boil in a small saucepan. Add the couscous, cover, and remove from the heat. Let stand 5 minutes, then fluff with a fork.

2 Meanwhile, cut a thin slice from the top of each tomato and reserve. With a spoon, carefully scoop out the seeds and pulp, leaving a tomato shell. Save the tomato pulp for soups or sauces.

3 Heat the oil in a large nonstick skillet over high heat. Add the zucchini, onion, bell pepper, and basil; cook, stirring frequently, until crisp-tender, about 5 minutes. Add the beans and tomato sauce; cook until slightly thickened, about 2 minutes. Remove from the heat and stir in the couscous, feta, and the remaining ½ teaspoon salt and ⅛ teaspoon pepper. Spoon about ¾ cup filling into each tomato shell and cover with the reserved tomato tops.

PER SERVING (1 stuffed tomato): 178 Cal, 3 g Fat, 1 g Sat Fat, 0 g Trans Fat, 3 mg Chol, 429 mg Sod, 30 g Carb, 7 g Fib, 9 g Prot, 110 mg Calc. **POINTS** value: **3.**

EXPRESS LANE If you're looking at a hectic schedule, this light entrée can be made a day ahead—just cover the stuffed tomatoes with plastic wrap before refrigerating. Or, for the best-looking presentation, refrigerate the tomato shells and filling separately, and stuff the tomatoes just before serving. For an extra 1 *POINT* value, serve with 1 long or 2 short breadsticks.

½ cup water

¾ teaspoon salt

¼ teaspoon freshly ground pepper

⅓ cup whole-wheat couscous

6 (7-ounce) beefsteak tomatoes

1 tablespoon extra-virgin olive oil

1 small zucchini, cut into ¼-inch dice (about 1 cup)

1 small onion, chopped

½ small red bell pepper, seeded and diced

1 teaspoon dried basil

1 (15½-ounce) can great northern beans, rinsed and drained

1 (8-ounce) can tomato sauce (no salt added)

⅓ cup crumbled fat-free feta cheese

Couscous-Stuffed Tomatoes

Stuffed Zucchini Boats

HANDS-ON PREP **5 MIN**
COOK **15 MIN**
SERVES **4**

1 Preheat the oven to 450°F. Spray an 8-inch square baking dish with nonstick spray.

2 Meanwhile, cut each zucchini in half lengthwise. With a small spoon, scoop out most of the flesh, leaving a ¼-inch border all around. Heat 1 cup water to a boil in a large skillet; add the zucchini shells and cook, covered, until slightly softened, about 3 minutes; drain and set aside on paper towels.

3 Meanwhile, heat the oil in a large nonstick skillet over medium-high heat. Add the onions and cook, stirring occasionally, until softened, about 4 minutes. Add the spinach, bread crumbs, nutmeg, and pepper; cook, stirring, until heated through, about 2 minutes.

4 Stuff the spinach mixture into the zucchini shells; sprinkle each with 1 tablespoon of the cheese. Place the zucchini in the baking dish and bake until heated through and lightly browned on top, about 6 minutes.

PER SERVING (1 piece): 121 Cal, 6 g Fat, 2 g Sat Fat, 0 g Trans Fat, 5 mg Chol, 215 mg Sod, 13 g Carb, 3 g Fib, 6 g Prot, 184 mg Calc. *POINTS* value: *2.*

EXPRESS LANE We use frozen chopped onions in this recipe to save chopping time. Be aware that as they begin to thaw in the skillet they first give off water before they start to brown. Also, don't discard the zucchini flesh; place in an airtight container in the refrigerator for up to 2 days. You can add it to soups or stews if you like.

2 **small to medium zucchini (about ¼ pound each)**

1 **tablespoon** olive oil

1 **cup frozen chopped onions**

1 **(10-ounce)** box frozen chopped spinach, **thawed and squeezed dry**

¼ **cup dried seasoned bread crumbs**

Large pinch nutmeg

Large pinch coarsely ground pepper

4 **tablespoons** shredded Parmesan cheese

Curried Lentils over Couscous

1 Bring ¾ cup + 2 tablespoons of the water, ½ teaspoon of the salt, and ⅛ teaspoon of the pepper to a boil in a small saucepan. Add the couscous, cover, and remove from the heat. Let stand 5 minutes, then fluff with a fork.

2 Meanwhile, heat the oil in a large nonstick skillet over high heat. Add the onion, carrot, celery, ginger, garlic, and curry powder; cook, stirring frequently, until the vegetables start to soften, about 5 minutes. Add the tomato and cook until just wilted, about 2 minutes. Stir in the lentils, raisins, the remaining ¼ cup water, and the remaining ¼ teaspoon salt and ⅛ teaspoon pepper; cook until hot and the water evaporates, about 3 minutes. Serve over the couscous.

PER SERVING (½ cup couscous and ⅔ cup lentil mixture): 308 Cal, 5 g Fat, 0 g Sat Fat, 0 g Trans Fat, 0 mg Chol, 645 mg Sod, 59 g Carb, 9 g Fib, 13 g Prot, 59 mg Calc. **POINTS** value: **6.**

FOOD NOTE If you want to prepare this recipe but you're following the **Core Plan**, simply omit the raisins (and decrease the *POINTS* value for each serving by 1).

1 cup + 2 tablespoons water

¾ teaspoon salt

¼ teaspoon freshly ground pepper

¾ cup whole-wheat couscous

1 tablespoon canola oil

1 onion, thinly sliced

1 carrot, chopped

1 celery stalk, chopped

1 tablespoon grated peeled fresh ginger

2 garlic cloves, minced

1 teaspoon curry powder

1 medium tomato, chopped

1 (15½-ounce) can lentils, rinsed and drained

½ cup raisins

Quick Desserts

CHAPTER 7

Caramelized Pineapple with Coconut Sorbet and Toasted Almonds

HANDS-ON PREP **10 MIN**
COOK **5 MIN**
SERVES **4**

1 Preheat the broiler. Spray a baking sheet with nonstick cooking spray.

2 Arrange the pineapple slices on the pan in a single layer. Sprinkle the pineapple evenly with the sugar and broil 5 inches from the heat until lightly browned, about 6 minutes.

3 Meanwhile, place the nuts in a dry skillet over medium-high heat. Cook, shaking the pan constantly, until lightly toasted, about 4 minutes. Turn the nuts onto a plate to cool.

4 Place 3 slices of pineapple on each of 4 dessert plates. Top each with $\frac{1}{3}$ cup of sorbet and 1 tablespoon of almonds. Serve at once.

PER SERVING (1 plate): 228 Cal, 5 g Fat, 2 g Sat Fat, 0 g Trans Fat, 1 mg Chol, 20 mg Sod, 47 g Carb, 3 g Fib, 2 g Prot, 36 mg Calc. **POINTS** value: **4.**

EXPRESS LANE The real time-saver here is using peeled, cored pineapples. Look for them in the produce section of your supermarket. If you can't find them, substitute a well-drained 20-ounce can of sliced pineapple in juice.

1 peeled, cored pineapple, (18-ounces) cut in 12 slices

3 tablespoons packed light brown sugar

$\frac{1}{4}$ **cup** sliced almonds

1$\frac{1}{3}$ **cups** coconut sorbet

Cranberry-Raisin Rice Pudding

HANDS-ON PREP **10 MIN**
COOK **10 MIN**
SERVES **6**

1 Combine the rice, milk, sugar, raisins, and cranberries in a medium saucepan. Bring the mixture to a boil over high heat. Reduce the heat and simmer, stirring occasionally, until the mixture thickens slightly, about 5 minutes.

2 Remove the pan from the heat, then stir in the almond extract and cinnamon. Serve at once, let cool to room temperature, or cover and refrigerate and serve cold.

PER SERVING (scant ½ cup): 202 Cal, 2 g Fat, 1 g Sat Fat, 0 g Trans Fat, 5 mg Chol, 213 mg Sod, 43 g Carb, 3 g Fib, 4 g Prot, 79 mg Calc. **POINTS** value: **4.**

GOOD IDEA Rice pudding is a great way to use leftover brown rice. If you have none, try picking up a container from your local Chinese restaurant the day before you plan on preparing the recipe.

2 **cups cooked brown rice**

1½ **cups reduced-fat (2%) milk**

½ **cup sugar**

¼ **cup raisins**

¼ **cup dried cranberries**

¼ **teaspoon almond extract**

¼ **teaspoon cinnamon**

Chocolate Cherry Pudding

Chocolate Cherry Pudding

HANDS-ON PREP **10 MIN**
COOK **10 MIN**
SERVES **6**

1 Combine the milk, sugar, cocoa powder, and cornstarch in a medium saucepan over medium-high heat. Cook, stirring constantly, until the mixture bubbles and thickens, about 10 minutes.

2 Remove the pan from the heat and stir in the chocolate until it melts. Stir in the cherries, vanilla extract, and almond extract.

3 Divide the pudding among 6 bowls and serve at once, let cool to room temperature, or chill.

PER SERVING (about ½ cup): 180 Cal, 4 g Fat, 2 g Sat Fat, 0 g Trans Fat, 2 mg Chol, 66 mg Sod, 35 g Carb, 3 g Fib, 6 g Prot, 165 mg Calc. **POINTS** value: **3.**

EXPRESS LANE Double the recipe and refrigerate half the pudding for an instant chilled dessert the next day. Just press plastic wrap directly onto the pudding before refrigerating to prevent a skin from forming.

3 **cups fat-free milk**

½ **cup sugar**

⅓ **cup unsweetened cocoa powder**

3 **tablespoons cornstarch**

1 **ounce unsweetened chocolate, finely chopped**

¼ **cup dried cherries**

½ **teaspoon vanilla extract**

½ **teaspoon almond extract**

Crêpes with Honeyed Sour Cream and Fresh Berries

HANDS-ON PREP **15 MIN**
COOK **2 MIN**
SERVES **4**

1 Combine the sour cream, honey, and orange zest in a small bowl; mix well.

2 Combine the strawberries, blueberries, orange juice, and sugar in a medium nonstick skillet over high heat. Cook until warm and slightly softened, about 2 minutes; remove from the heat.

3 Arrange 1 crêpe on each of 4 plates. Spoon 1 tablespoon of the sour cream mixture down the center of each crêpe; top each with ½ cup of the fruit, then fold the edges of the crêpes over the filling. Spoon the remaining fruit over the crêpes. Serve at once.

PER SERVING (1 filled crêpe): 192 Cal, 5 g Fat, 2 g Sat Fat, 1 g Trans Fat, 38 mg Chol, 188 mg Sod, 34 g Carb, 2 g Fib, 6 g Prot, 92 mg Calc. **POINTS** value: **4.**

FOOD NOTE Thankfully, there are now several brands of crêpes available in the supermarket that both taste good and are low in fat. Look for them in the produce or dairy section.

¼ **cup** light sour cream

1 **tablespoon** honey

1 **teaspoon** grated orange zest

12 **fresh strawberries, stems removed, berries quartered**

1 **(6-ounce) container fresh blueberries**

2 **tablespoons orange juice**

1 **tablespoon** sugar

4 **ready-to-use crêpes**

Angel Food Cake with Mixed Berries and Raspberry Sauce

HANDS-ON PREP **20 MIN**
COOK **NONE**
SERVES **6**

1 Combine the strawberries, blackberries, blueberries, 2 tablespoons of the sugar, and 2 teaspoons of the lemon juice in a bowl; toss well.

2 Combine the remaining ½ cup sugar and 1 tablespoon lemon juice with the raspberries in a blender. Process on high speed until smooth, 1–2 minutes. Strain the sauce into a bowl through a wire-mesh sieve, pressing with a rubber spatula; discard the seeds.

3 To assemble, spoon about 3 tablespoons of the sauce onto each of 6 dessert plates. Place a wedge of cake on top of the sauce then spoon on ⅔ cup of the mixed berry mixture.

PER SERVING (1 plate): 275 Cal, 1 g Fat, 0 g Sat Fat, 0 g Trans Fat, 0 mg Chol, 321 mg Sod, 66 g Carb, 5 g Fib, 4 g Prot, 33 mg Calc. *POINTS* value: *5.*

FOOD NOTE **If you use frozen raspberries to make the sauce, allow about 20 minutes for them to thaw at room temperature.**

1 **pint** fresh **strawberries, stems removed, berries quartered**

1 **(6-ounce) container** fresh **blackberries**

1 **(6-ounce) container** fresh **blueberries**

½ **cup + 2 tablespoons** sugar

1 **tablespoon + 2 teaspoons** fresh **lemon juice**

2 **(6-ounce) containers** fresh **raspberries, or 2 cups thawed frozen**

1 **(9-ounce)** store-bought **angel food cake, cut into 6 wedges**

Figs with Greek Yogurt, Honey, and Walnuts

HANDS-ON PREP **10 MIN**
COOK **5 MIN**
SERVES **4**

1 Combine the figs and orange juice in a small saucepan over high heat; bring to a boil. Remove the pan from the heat and let stand 5 minutes. Drain, then divide the figs among 4 bowls.

2 Meanwhile, heat the nuts in a dry skillet over medium-high heat. Cook, shaking the pan constantly, until lightly toasted, 4–5 minutes. Remove the skillet from the heat.

3 Combine the yogurt and milk in a bowl; stir until smooth. Spoon the yogurt evenly over the figs. Top each bowl with 1 tablespoon of the toasted walnuts and 1 tablespoon of the honey.

PER SERVING (1 bowl): 267 Cal, 5 g Fat, 1 g Sat Fat, 0 g Trans Fat, 3 mg Chol, 103 mg Sod, 49 g Carb, 4 g Fib, 10 g Prot, 302 mg Calc. **POINTS** value: **5.**

FOOD NOTE Greek-style yogurt is thicker, creamier, and slightly tangier than the American yogurts we are accustomed to. If you can't find it in a specialty store or supermarket's dairy section, you can make your own yogurt cheese which is a reasonable substitute. To make yogurt cheese, spoon 2 cups plain fat-free yogurt into a sieve lined with a damp paper towel; place over a bowl. Refrigerate, covered, 1½ hours or overnight. Discard the liquid in the bowl. Makes 1 cup yogurt cheese.

12 **Calimyrna dried figs, stems removed, figs quartered**

¾ **cup orange juice**

¼ **cup coarsely chopped walnuts**

1 **cup Greek-style fat-free yogurt**

2 **tablespoons skim milk**

¼ **cup honey**

Figs with Greek Yogurt,
Honey, and Walnuts

Two-Fruit Fool

HANDS-ON PREP **10 MIN**
COOK **NONE**
SERVES **4**

1 Divide the whipped topping between 2 bowls. With a rubber spatula gently fold the blueberry preserves into 1 bowl of the topping. Fold the apricot into the other bowl.

2 Gently spoon the blueberry mixture evenly into the bottom of 4 glass sundae dishes. Spoon the apricot mixture evenly onto the blueberry mixture. Serve at once or refrigerate until ready to serve.

PER SERVING (1 dish): 147 Cal, 1 g Fat, 1 g Sat Fat, 0 g Trans Fat, 0 mg Chol, 35 mg Sod, 36 g Carb, 1 g Fib, 0 g Prot, 6 mg Calc. **POINTS** value: **3.**

TRY IT A fool is an old English dessert that combines a cooked fruit puree and whipped cream. Originally the fruit of the day was gooseberries, but modern times have opened this dessert up to all sorts of interpretations, like this speedy version with fruit preserves.

1 (8-ounce) container frozen fat-free nondairy whipped topping, thawed

3 tablespoons blueberry preserves

3 tablespoons apricot preserves

Honeydew Soup

HANDS-ON PREP **10 MIN**
COOK **NONE**
SERVES **4**

Combine the honeydew, sugar, lemon juice, mint, and lemon zest in a blender; process on high speed until pureed. Transfer the mixture to a large bowl and serve at once, garnished with the chopped cantaloupe, if using. Or cover and refrigerate for up to 24 hours and serve chilled.

PER SERVING (1 cup): 95 Cal, 0 g Fat, 0 g Sat Fat, 0 g Trans Fat, 0 mg Chol, 18 mg Sod, 25 g Carb, 1 g Fib, 1 g Prot, 13 mg Calc. **POINTS** value: *2.*

GOOD IDEA Try substituting other melons such as cantaloupe, galia (a cross between honeydew and cantaloupe melons, but a bit more expensive), or Crenshaw melon for a simple variation. If you choose a Crenshaw melon, look for one with yellow, rather than creamy white, skin—the yellow has better flavor.

½ **medium honeydew melon, cubed (about 5 cups)**

3 **tablespoons sugar**

2 **tablespoons fresh lemon juice**

2 **tablespoons chopped fresh mint**

1 **teaspoon grated lemon zest**

½ **cup finely chopped cantaloupe or honeydew (optional for garnish)**

Mixed Melons with Peppery Minted Lime Syrup

HANDS-ON PREP **10 MIN**
COOK **5 MIN**
SERVES **4**

1 Combine the sugar, water, lime juice, and cayenne in a small saucepan over high heat and bring to a boil. Boil, until the mixture is syrupy, about 5 minutes. Remove the pan from the heat, then stir in the mint and lime zest; let stand about 2 minutes.

2 Combine the honeydew, watermelon, and cantaloupe in a large bowl. Pour the syrup mixture over the fruit and toss well. Serve at once or cover and refrigerate overnight and serve chilled.

PER SERVING (1½ cups): 182 Cal, 1 g Fat, 0 g Sat Fat, 0 g Trans Fat, 0 mg Chol, 21 mg Sod, 46 g Carb, 2 g Fib, 2 g Prot, 25 mg Calc. **POINTS** value: **3.**

EXPRESS LANE For speediest prep, look for precut melon in the produce section of your local supermarket or at the salad bar.

½ **cup sugar**

½ **cup water**

3 **tablespoons** fresh lime juice

⅛ **teaspoon** cayenne

2 **tablespoons chopped fresh mint**

2 **teaspoons** grated lime zest

2 **cups cubed** honeydew melon (about ¾ pound)

2 **cups cubed** seedless watermelon (about ¾ pound)

2 **cups cubed** cantaloupe (about ¾ pound)

Mango-Strawberry Shakes

HANDS-ON PREP **10 MIN**
COOK **NONE**
SERVES **4**

Combine the mangoes, strawberries, soy milk, yogurt, honey, vanilla, and ice cubes in a blender. Process on high speed until smooth, 1–2 minutes. Divide among 4 glasses and serve at once.

PER SERVING (1 cup): 203 Cal, 2 g Fat, 0 g Sat Fat, 0 g Trans Fat, 1 mg Chol, 74 mg Sod, 44 g Carb, 4 g Fib, 6 g Prot, 190 mg Calc. **POINTS** value: **3.**

GOOD IDEA For intense tropical flavor, look for extra-ripe mangoes that are soft to the touch. If you prefer, substitute 1½ cups of frozen strawberries for the fresh and eliminate the ice cubes.

2 ripe mangoes, peeled, seeded, and cubed

1 pint fresh strawberries, stemmed

1 cup vanilla soy milk

1 cup vanilla fat-free yogurt

1 tablespoon honey

½ teaspoon vanilla extract

4 ice cubes

Old-Time Vanilla Malt

Old-Time Vanilla Malt

HANDS-ON PREP **10 MIN**
COOK **NONE**
SERVES **4**

Combine the ice cream, milk, malt powder, and syrup in a blender. Process on high speed until thick and smooth, about 1 minute. Pour into 4 tall slim glasses and serve with extra-long straws.

PER SERVING (¾ cup): 184 Cal, 5 g Fat, 3 g Sat Fat, 0 g Trans Fat, 25 mg Chol, 107 mg Sod, 28 g Carb, 0 g Fib, 6 g Prot, 212 mg Calc. **POINTS** value: **4.**

FOOD NOTE You can buy vanilla syrup in bottles in coffee shops and specialty stores. If you have extra, it's great for flavoring coffees or lattes.

2 cups vanilla low-fat (light) ice cream

1½ cups skim milk

2 tablespoons malt powder

2 tablespoons vanilla syrup

Microwave Potato Nachos, page 21

Dry and Liquid Measurement Equivalents

If you are converting the recipes in this book to metric measurements, use the following chart as a guide.

TEASPOONS	TABLESPOONS	CUPS	FLUID OUNCES
3 teaspoons	1 tablespoon		½ fluid ounce
6 teaspoons	2 tablespoons	⅛ cup	1 fluid ounce
8 teaspoons	2 tablespoons plus 2 teaspoons	⅙ cup	
12 teaspoons	4 tablespoons	¼ cup	2 fluid ounces
15 teaspoons	5 tablespoons	⅓ cup minus 1 teaspoon	
16 teaspoons	5 tablespoons plus 1 teaspoon	⅓ cup	
18 teaspoons	6 tablespoons	¼ cup plus 2 tablespoons	3 fluid ounces
24 teaspoons	8 tablespoons	½ cup	4 fluid ounces
30 teaspoons	10 tablespoons	½ cup plus 2 tablespoons	5 fluid ounces
32 teaspoons	10 tablespoons plus 2 teaspoons	⅔ cup	
36 teaspoons	12 tablespoons	¾ cup	6 fluid ounces
42 teaspoons	14 tablespoons	1 cup minus 2 tablespoons	7 fluid ounces
45 teaspoons	15 tablespoons	1 cup minus 1 tablespoon	
48 teaspoons	16 tablespoons	1 cup	8 fluid ounces

VOLUME	
¼ teaspoon	1 milliliter
½ teaspoon	2 milliliters
1 teaspoon	5 milliliters
1 tablespoon	15 milliliters
2 tablespoons	30 milliliters
3 tablespoons	45 milliliters
¼ cup	60 milliliters
⅓ cup	80 milliliters
½ cup	120 milliliters
⅔ cup	160 milliliters
¾ cup	175 milliliters
1 cup	240 milliliters
1 quart	950 milliliters

LENGTH	
1 inch	25 millimeters
1 inch	2.5 centimeters

WEIGHT	
1 ounce	30 grams
¼ pound	120 grams
½ pound	240 grams
1 pound	480 grams

OVEN TEMPERATURE			
250°F	120°C	400°F	200°C
275°F	140°C	425°F	220°C
300°F	150°C	450°F	230°C
325°F	160°C	475°F	250°C
350°F	180°C	500°F	260°C
375°F	190°C	525°F	270°C

NOTE: Measurement of less than ⅛ teaspoon is considered a dash or a pinch. Metric volume measurements are approximate.

Index

POINTS value Recipe Index

Chicken Sausages Provençal on Polenta, 98

Chicken with Wild Mushroom-Marsala Sauce, 84

Chinese Meatballs with Bok Choy, 108

Cornmeal-Crusted Chicken with Peach Salsa, 86

Cranberry Pork Tenderloin with Squash Puree, 68

Dilled Tuna Baguette, 50

Duck Tostados, 115

Figs with Greek Yogurt, Honey, and Walnuts, 180

Moroccan Chicken and Couscous Soup, 92

Oatmeal Brûlée, 42

Orzo "Risotto" with Asparagus, Tomatoes, and Cheese, 159

Oven-Fried Pork Chops, 74

Pan-Seared Salmon with Balsamic Drizzle, 121

Parmesan-Crusted Turkey with Tomato-Lemon Sauté, 107

Pressure Cooker Lamb Tagine, 80

Pressure-Cooked Sweet Rice Porridge, 45

Salade aux Lardons, 76

Scallop Miso Bowl with Soba Noodles and Spinach, 138

Scrambled Tortilla Eggs with Taco Sauce, 32

Seven-Layer Salad, 66

Steak au Poivre, 55

Tofu Lo Mein, 152

Turkey Cutlets with Cranberry-Nut Topping, 105

Tuscan Chicken Sausage Stew, 97

Warm Chicken, Apple, and Curried Couscous Salad, 95

Yucatan Chicken and Tortilla Soup, 91

6 *POINTS* value

Beef Orzo Soup, 60

Blue Cheese Polenta with Sautéed Onions, 158

Breakfast Burrito, 34

Cuban Black Beans and Rice, 163

Curried Lentils over Couscous, 171

Easy Pork Sauté

Gnocchi with Parsley Pesto, 160

Hummus Bruschetta with Mediterranean Salad, 167

Macaroni and Cheese, 157

Microwave-Poached Salmon with Lemon-Dill Sauce, 120

Pasta Bolognese with Mushrooms, 103

Pasta Moussaka, 81

Red Thai Chicken Curry with Cauliflower, 90

Thai Coconut-Chicken Soup, 99

7 *POINTS* value

Chicken Quesadillas with Creamy Salsa, 94

Clams Capellini with Fresh Tomatoes, 146

Curried Turkey Burger with Rice, 110

Escarole with Beans and Pasta, 165

Meatless Fettuccine Bolognese, 154

Mexican Sloppy Joe Tortilla Cups, 100

Pasta with Sausage, Spinach, and Pine Nuts, 112

Turkish Turkey Burger, 109

Tuscan "Pitzas", 153

8 *POINTS* value

French Chicken Burger, 102

Mussels in Spicy Tomato Sauce with Fresh Linguine, 144

9 *POINTS* value

Tuna, Roasted Pepper, and Tzatziki Sandwiches, 122

Notes

Notes

Notes

Notes

Notes